A CULINARY JOURNEY THROUGH TEXAS HISTORY

A State Historic Sites Cookbook

TEXAS HISTORICAL COMMISSION

REAL PLACES TELLING REAL STORIES

ISBN: 979-8-218-37383-2

Texas Historical Commission
Historic Sites Division
P.O. Box 12276
Austin, TX 78711
512-463-6100
thc@thc.texas.gov

RESEARCH, WRITING, AND EDITING

Hal Simon, Chief of Interpretation, Historic Sites
Sara Nezamabadi, Exhibit & Interpretive Design Specialist, Historic Sites
Jonathan McMahon, Interpretive Writing Specialist, Historic Sites
Shelley Wong, Regional Retail Development Manager, Historic Sites
Thomas Wilhelm, Director of Earned Revenue, Historic Sites
Inez Wolins, Assistant Deputy Executive Director of Historic Sites, Historic Sites
Joseph Bell, Executive Director, Texas Historical Commission

DESIGN AND LAYOUT

Sara Nezamabadi, Exhibit & Interpretive Design Specialist, Historic Sites

---

Thank you to all state historic sites' staff for contributing your knowledge and foodways programming photographs for this cookbook.

ACKNOWLEDGMENTS

This collection would not have been possible without the dedication of many colleagues across our Texas State Historic Sites. Each recipe carries with it the work of staff and volunteers who have cared for collections, recorded oral histories, and welcomed visitors into kitchens and dining rooms where traditions were first made.

I am especially grateful to those whose scholarship and generosity enriched these pages. Gratitude is extended to our outstanding team at the Texas Historical Commission, whose collaboration made this project a reality:

Commissioner Monica Zárate Burdett for suggesting this project and assisting in the review of all recipes once transcribed.

Shelley Wong for initiating the groundwork that launched the project and for her writing and research for this cookbook.

Inez Wolins, Historic Sites Assistant Deputy Executive Director, for her encouragement, guidance, and assistance in the creation and editing of the cookbook.

Hal Simon, Historic Sites Chief of Interpretation, for researching, transcribing, adapting, editing the historic recipes, and for writing the appendices.

Sara Nezamabadi, Exhibit & Interpretive Design Specialist, for her editing, research, and graphic design of the artwork and photographs for the overall layout and design.

Jonathan McMahon, Interpretive Writing Specialist, for researching, reviewing, and writing the text.

Thomas Wilhelm, Director of Earned Revenue, for book production and publication.

Special thanks to the Site Managers and their staff at our Historic Sites, whose recipe submissions have helped us tell the tale of Texas cuisine.

We also owe a debt to those who preserved diaries, family cookbooks, and community archives, assuring that a grandmother's cornbread or a soldier's ration could be remembered with accuracy and care. The recipes gathered here are more than instructions for a meal; they are fragments of lived experience, sustained by the commitment of those who continue to keep history alive at our sites and within our communities.

Joseph Bell
Texas Historical Commission, Executive Director
State Historic Preservation Officer

Volunteer interpreter conducting foodways programming in the officer's quarters kitchen, Fort McKavett State Historic Site, Fort McKavett, Texas.

Table of Contents

INTRODUCTION

Texas cuisine as we know it is the product of the ingredients, cooking techniques, and traditions brought to the state by the various peoples who have lived on this land which combined into the melting pot that is our state today. Our cuisine has elements drawn from Indigenous people, Hispanic culture, German, French, English, Jewish, and other European settlers, and Americans from the Deep South, Upper Midwest, and Mid-Atlantic seaboard.

Throughout the 19th and early 20th centuries recipes were often passed along in households verbally, in handwritten cookbooks, and as time progressed through publications from periodicals to dedicated cookbooks. More than 1,500 cookbooks were published in the United States between 1800 and 1930, and many of these found their way into the households of Texans from every walk of life. Cookbooks became increasingly popular as literacy rates rose, and the middle class grew, from the end of the Civil War through the post WWII era. They played a vital role in creating the culinary culture we know and influencing how we cook and eat through the current day.

The earliest Texans were the Indigenous peoples of the east Texas Piney Woods, the Blackland Prairie, and arid West Texas. They foraged wild vegetables and edible plants and hunted the many game animals both large and small that proliferated their specific areas. Some non-nomadic tribes like the Caddo also engaged in organized agriculture raising crops like corn, beans, and squash. Their cooking would have primarily been over open fires in clay pots or on earthenware comals. They would also have preserved food by drying it for storage in large pots or by preserving it in pots of bear or buffalo fat.

Early Spanish and Mexican Texas saw the introduction of hornos (domed baking ovens) and agujeros para guiso (stew-hole stoves) which were permanent raised structures in kitchens that had a series of holes onto which pots were fitted . They were heated by a fire built in an adjacent firebox. The Spanish also first introduced wheat and wheat flour into early Texas, prior to which the Indigenous peoples would have use corn as their major flour and meal resource. Cattle, pigs, and domesticated chickens were also first introduced into the area by the Spanish. The Spanish soon began including local produce and spices into their food, helping to create what we now know of as Mexican foods.

American and European immigrants initially cooked in outdoor fire pits or in open-hearth fireplaces they constructed. Most early Texas homes located the kitchen hearth in a separate structure to keep cooking odors and heat out of their home during the hot Texas summers. Cast iron stoves, brought in by wagon freight, were introduced into Texas by the mid-1830s, but were luxuries few early families could initially afford. These immigrants also brought their own food traditions which derived from the deep South, upper Midwest, Eastern seaboard, or their European counties of origin.

African culinary practices significantly influenced 19th-century American cuisine, particularly in the South, through the introduction of new ingredients and techniques by enslaved Africans. These influences shaped dishes like gumbo and jambalaya and contributed to the development of Southern barbecue styles. These enslaved laborers brought their knowledge of crops like rice, okra, black-eyed peas, and various spices, which became staples in American cuisine, particularly in the Southern States including Texas.

Our Texas cuisine today is a true melting pot of all these different cultural influences and gives our state its distinctive flavors that we all enjoy. This Historic Sites Cookbook contains recipes used across the different regions of our state from prior to European contact up through the 1950s.

Welcome to a culinary tour of Texas history, pull up a chair and dig in!

Hal Simon
Chief of Interpretation
Texas Historical Commission, Historic Sites

NOTES ON HISTORIC RECIPES

All the historic recipes in this cookbook that pre-date the 20th century have been redacted (adapted) from their original paragraph format without a separate ingredients list into a modern recipe format. Prior to the mid-19th century, the term applied to the directions for cooking was "receipt" instead of "recipe". In addition, many of the measurements listed in the original recipes may be in terms with which modern cooks are unfamiliar.

A special Appendix has been included at the back of the book for the reader to see how measurement terms change over time and finally become standardized into those we all use today. Historical notes have been included with each recipe to give historical context and information about their use in Texas.

POTATOES STEWED WHOLE.

Boil two dozen small new potatoes, with some salt. Put into a stew-pan a piece of butter rolled in flour, half the peel of a lemon grated, half a nutmeg grated, some salt, two or three lumps of sugar, and three tea-spoonfuls of sweet oil. Lay the potatoes in this mixture, squeeze over them the juice of a lemon, and let them stew gently about ten minutes.

OYSTER SOUP.

Take two hundred oysters from their liquor, strain it and put it into a saucepan to simmer; rub a spoonful of flour and two large spoonsful of butter together, a very little cayenne, half a teaspoonful of salt, some grated nutmeg or mace, but not both, and a teaspoonful of allspice, whole; set this on the fire for ten minutes, and then pour in a pint of good cream; let this simmer five minutes, and then add the oysters. A few pieces of celery gives a very nice flavour. Serve hot. Do not more than scald the oysters, as they shrink and become hard by cooking.

Chief of Interpretation, Hal Simon, performing foodways programming in the kitchen at French Legation State Historic Site, Austin, Texas.

Indigenous and Hispanic Texas

1800-1836

When the first group of Spanish explorers arrived in Texas in 1528, they found a land that had already been inhabited for at least 20,000 years. Long before their arrival, native people had a varied diet. They had mastered agriculture and raised various crops, particularly corn, beans, and squash. They also cultivated various wild plants like persimmons, mustang grapes, and pecans. Acorns and mesquite pods were gathered and ground into flour. Proteins included pronghorns, deer, rabbits, turkeys, quails, catfish, turtles, freshwater mussels, crawfish, and land snails.

The Spanish brought their own food culture to the region, introducing domesticated animals like pigs, goats, cattle, chickens, and sheep. They also introduced certain fruits and vegetables, such as citrus, bananas, wheat, sugarcane, rice, and onions. The use of dairy products was another culinary concept that was mostly unknown in the Americas before European colonization. These European foodways blended with indigenous staples, creating a foundation for a new culinary era in the Americas.

One of the most significant contributions from this era is barbacoa, a method of cooking meat in an underground pit. This cooking style, which dates back at least 8,000 years in Texas, was adopted and refined by both Indigenous peoples and settlers. The use of earthen ovens, where food was placed on hot coals, covered, and cooked for hours or days, became an enduring tradition. Today, this method continues with modern barbecue pitmasters cooking barbacoa, reflecting the deep cultural roots of Texas cuisine.

By the early 19th century, Texas was part of Spain and, later, Mexico. The use of tortillas, tamales, and cornmeal-based dishes continued as part of daily life, reflecting Native American agricultural practices. As indigenous ingredients like corn, chili peppers, and beans were incorporated into European diets, a distinct culinary fusion began to form. This era set the stage for the food culture that would evolve as Texas transitioned from Mexican to Anglo-American control.

When Mexico gained independence from Spain in 1821, it ended the chance of Spain being a threat to the United States. It also opened up new opportunities for trade and expansion.
Just a year later, the Santa Fe Trail connected the Mexican region of Nuevo Mexico with St. Louis, Missouri. This trail helped grow trade between the two countries, especially as Americans began moving to Texas and the American West.

In 1834, the Mexican government grew worried because so many Anglo-Americans were settling in Texas so quickly. To better understand the situation, Mexican Col. Juan N. Almonte was sent to scout the area. One subject Almonte reported on was the food people were eating. Mexicans mostly ate tortillas, beef, venison, chicken, eggs, cheese, and milk. Sometimes they also had bread, chocolate, coffee, tea, and sugar. Anglo-Americans, on the other hand, usually ate bacon, cornbread, coffee sweetened with honey, butter, buttermilk, and sometimes crackers. Anglos rarely ate beef, except in places like Nacogdoches and San Antonio, where cattle were regularly slaughtered.

Texas cuisine has deep indigenous roots built on agricultural knowledge and wild resources. Spanish colonization introduced new animals, crops, and culinary techniques, blending European and Native traditions to help contribute to a new Mexican culture. Mexican food was well-established when Americans and the enslaved peoples, who came with them, added the final layers to the culinary landscape of the period. These layered influences from Native, Spanish, Mexican, and Anglo-American cultures shaped the food traditions that define Texas cuisine today.

Kitchen at the French Legation State Historic Site, Austin, Texas.

Starters and Small Bites

BIRD PEPPER SALSA

PRESIDIO LA BAHÍA STATE HISTORIC SITE

Historical Note:

While this is a contemporary recipe, the chili pequin is the only pepper native to North America. In fact, it is considered to be the Official Native Pepper of Texas. It gets its name "bird pepper" from the fact that birds, who are not sensitive to the extremely hot taste of capsaicin, love to eat the fruits, which are high in Vitamins A and C. They are hotter than a jalapeño, milder than a habanero.

INGREDIENTS:

3 Roma tomatoes
5-6 chili pequins, fresh or dried
4 oz. tomato sauce
½ tsp. fresh garlic, chopped
½ medium white onion
½ tsp. cumin
1 jalapeño
1-2 T. of chopped cilantro

PROCESS:

Mix all the ingredients together in a molcajete or food processor and grind to your desired texture. This recipe will produce a medium heat salsa that is great on anything you use salsa for!

FRIED TOMATOES
ACTON STATE HISTORIC SITE

Historical Note:

Recipe adapted from ***The Kentucky Housewife****, Lettice Bryan,1839.*

INGREDIENTS:

4 or 5 large, ripe tomatoes
1-½ C. breadcrumbs
1 medium onion
Salt and pepper
Sufficient butter for frying

PROCESS:

Peel the tomatoes and cut them into thick slices. Season them with salt and pepper and dip each side of each slice in the breadcrumbs making sure to coat thoroughly. Melt the butter in a skillet until very hot and fry the tomato slices in it. Drain them on a paper towel and transfer them to a serving platter. Mince the onion and fry it in the same pan until it is caramelized and sprinkle them on top of the tomatoes. Serve them very warm.

MARY MARK'S CORN DODGERS

SAN FELIPE DE AUSTIN STATE HISTORIC SITE

Historical Note:

Mary Marks was an enslaved woman working as a waitress and cook at the Whitesides Hotel in San Felipe de Austin. One specific recipe commented on by town resident and memoirist Noah Smithwick, was her corn dodger recipe. Early Texans were accustomed to having corn or cornbread with practically every meal because of the abundance of the crop.

INGREDIENTS:

1¼" deep of canola oil, vegetable oil, or lard, (enough oil to cover a frying pan)
½ C. flour
1½ C. cornmeal
½ tsp. salt
½ tsp. baking powder
1 C. water
1 egg

PROCESS:

Heat a skillet with oil or fat on medium heat. While heating, mix together the flour, cornmeal, salt, and baking powder. Add water and egg to form a workable dough. Form pieces of dough 2-3" wide and about 1" thick. Fry evenly on both sides until done (2-4 minutes per side).

Below: Lead Interpreter and Educator, Nicole Shadle, cooking at San Felipe de Austin State Historic Site.

'MA' BYRD'S FAMOUS SHRIMP FRIED PIES

PORT ISABEL LIGHTHOUSE STATE HISTORIC SITE

Historical Note:

As a result of the dust bowl and depression of the 1930s, the Byrd family ended up in Port Isabel where Mr. Byrd found himself employed in the commercial fishing industry. Ma Byrd was known for her fried pies. Her Fried Shrimp Pie was so popular among friends and family that she was encouraged to enter the World's Championship Shrimp Cook-Off. She took 1st place in 1999!

INGREDIENTS:

1 C. chopped celery
1 C. chopped onion
1 C. chopped bell pepper
1 C. butter
2 ¼ C. flour, divided
2 C. milk
Creole Seasoning to taste
Chopped jalapeños
1 lb. cooked lump crab meat
1 lb. cooked, peeled, and de-veined Gulf wild-caught shrimp

CRUST:

⅓ C. butter
½ C. water
2 C. flour

PROCESS:

Filling: In a skillet, sauté celery, onions, and bell peppers in 1 cup of butter. When tender add 2 tablespoons of flour. Sauté until light brown. Add more butter if needed. Add 2 cups of milk. If too thick, add more milk. If too thin, add more flour. Season to taste with Creole Seasoning. Add chopped jalapeños, cooked crab meat, and chopped shrimp. Freeze mixture to harden.

Pie crust: Mix ⅓ cup of butter, ½ cup of water, and 2 cups of flour. Chill for 30 minutes. Roll pie crust. Cut 6 inches in diameter. Spoon (1 tablespoon) shrimp mixture in the middle of dough circle. Fold over and seal with a fork. Fry in hot oil until golden brown.

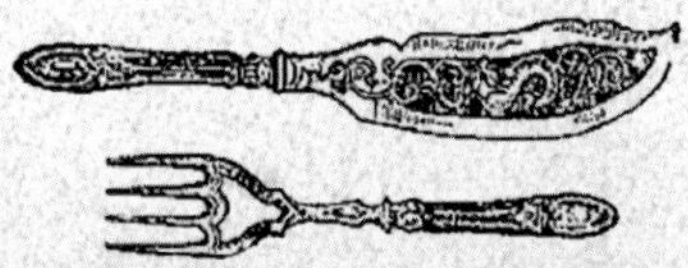

FISH CARVERS.

PELMENI

NATIONAL MUSEUM OF THE PACIFIC WAR STATE HISTORIC SITE

Historical Note:

Recipe from Robert Pennell, a Captain in the US Army in the Philippines, who served in the 3rd Battalion, 21st Infantry Regiment, Philippine Scouts during the attack on Bataan on the Philippine Islands. He received a Silver Star for his actions during the defense of Bataan. Recipes are from diaries kept by Pennell while he was in the Zentsuji Prisoner-of-War camp.

INGREDIENTS:

3 C. Buckwheat flour
1 tsp. Salt
1 T. Butter
1 T. Sugar
Optional: Pre-cooked meat
1 egg, hard-boiled
Nuts, jam, jelly, or fruit

PROCESS:

Make dough of buckwheat flour, salt, butter, and sugar (no yeast or baking powder). Roll to 48", and cut into 1" discs. Fill discs with finely chopped pre-cooked meat and chopped hard-boiled egg. Seal and cook by boiling in soup. Remove from soup when done and serve on the side. These are sometimes filled with nuts, jam, jelly, or fruit either boiled or fried.

POUNDED CHEESE

SAN FELIPE DE AUSTIN STATE HISTORIC SITE

Historical Note:

*Recipe adapted from **The Cook's Own Book**, Mrs. N. K. M. Lee 1832.*

INGREDIENTS:

1 lb medium cheddar cheese
2 oz. butter
Spices to your taste (black pepper, cayenne, curry powder, and dry mustard are all appropriate)
2-3 oz. sherry or port wine

PROCESS:

Cut the cheese into thin pieces or grate it. Add the butter and knead it together until it is very smooth, adding your choice of spices and the sherry or port as you go. Pack the mixture tightly in a jar or other desired container. It can be spread on bread or crackers to eat.

Right: Interpreter and Educator, Railey Tassin, cooking at Kreische Brewery State Historic Site, La Grange, Texas.

SPICY PORK RINDS

BUSH FAMILY HOME STATE HISTORIC SITE

Historical Note:

While on the campaign trail, George H. W. Bush reportedly identified pork rinds as being one of his favorite snacks. He often topped pork rinds with Tabasco sauce.

INGREDIENTS:

1 bag of pork rinds
Tabasco sauce

PROCESS:

Pork rinds can be eaten as a snack directly from the bag. They can also be crushed and used in recipes as a substitute for breadcrumbs. Pork rinds are often used as a cracker to scoop dip.

SPICY SPAM PARTY DIP

BUSH FAMILY HOME STATE HISTORIC SITE

Historical Note:

This recipe is from December 1958 Better Homes and Gardens magazine, and is typical of the types of party foods served during the years that the Bush family lived in their Midland, Texas home.

INGREDIENTS:

2 (8-ounce) packages cream cheese, softened
1 (12-ounce) can SPAM® Classic, grated
2 T. Worcestershire sauce
1 tsp. chunky tomato salsa
1 pinch ground red pepper (cayenne)
1 C. finely chopped green or red bell pepper
½ C. chopped celery
¼ C. chopped onion
2 T. chopped fresh cilantro

PROCESS:

In a medium bowl, combine cream cheese, SPAM® Classic, Worcestershire sauce, salsa and cayenne. Beat with electric mixer on medium speed until smooth. Stir in bell pepper, celery, onion and cilantro; cover. Refrigerate for 1 hour. Serve dip with crackers, chips and cut-up fresh vegetables.

Republic Era
1836-1846

The mid-1820s marked the arrival of Anglo-American settlers in Texas, encouraged by empresarios, who were colonial era land agents like Moses Austin and his son, Stephen F. Austin. In 1836, Texas declared its independence from Mexico, forming the Republic of Texas, which lasted until 1845 when the young nation joined the United States. Alongside Anglo settlers, a substantial number of enslaved Africans arrived, further broadening the foodways of the region. Dishes such as gumbo, sweet potatoes and yams, and other rice-based meals found their way into Texas kitchens, while techniques like deep-frying became more common, enriching the region's culinary landscape.

The blending of Indigenous, Spanish, Anglo, and African traditions during the Republic Era led to a distinctive food culture. Dishes and cooking methods from all over the world came together, reflecting the melting pot of the people who called Texas home. This era also marked the growth of Texas' agriculture, with cotton becoming the dominant cash crop but corn continued to play a key role in the local diet. Pork, became the most common protein consumed at the time, appeared in many recipes, and corn coffee, a staple for many Texans, reflects both agricultural practices and economic conditions of the era.

Food during the Republic period not only nourished the body but also carried the weight of Texas' evolving identity. The culinary traditions developed during this time laid the foundation for the state's future food culture, which would continue to evolve with the changing demographics and economy of the region.

Landmark Inn State Historic Site, Castroville, Texas.

Educator and Interpreter, Nathan Giles, working the cornfield at Barrington Living History Farm State Historic Site, Washington, Texas.

Salads and Dressings

CHICKEN SALAD
EISENHOWER BIRTHPLACE STATE HISTORIC SITE

Historical Note:

Recipe adapted from ***Practical American Cookery and Household Management****, Julia Corson,1886*

MAYONNAISE INGREDIENTS:

1 egg yolk
1 tsp. salt
1 Capful of vinegar
Pepper to taste
1 Capful of good salad oil

MAYONNAISE PROCESS:

To make the mayonnaise, put into an earthen bowl the yolk of a raw egg, a level teaspoonful of salt, a teaspoonful of vinegar, and a little pepper; stir these ingredients until they are smoothly mixed, and then gradually drop in a capful of good salad oil, adding it slowly, and stirring the mayonnaise constantly until it grows quite thick; then use a few drops of vinegar to thin it a little, and after that stir in more oil; proceed in this way until all the oil is used.

Chicken salad is sometimes made with celery instead of lettuce, and is usually garnished with hard-boiled eggs; cold boiled beets, capers, olives, and the small leaves of lettuce or celery are also used to garnish chicken salad.

CHICKEN SALAD INGREDIENTS:

1 pt. boiled or roasted chicken, cut in small pieces
1 large head of lettuce, thoroughly washed and torn into pieces
Salt and pepper to taste

SALAD PROCESS:

When ready to serve the salad, mix the lettuce and chicken in a salad bowl, season them lightly with salt, and pepper, pour the mayonnaise over the salad, and serve it at once.

FRENCH SALAD DRESSING

STARR FAMILY HOME STATE HISTORIC SITE

Historical Note:

Recipe adapted from ***Miss Parola's New Cook Book****, Maria Parola, 1882*

INGREDIENTS:

1 Saltspoonful (¼ tsp. of salt)
½ Saltspoonful of pepper (⅛ tsp.)
3 T. oil, divided
1 T. vinegar
A few drops of onion juice (optional)

PROCESS:

Put the salt and pepper in a cup, and add one tablespoonful of the oil. When thoroughly mixed, add the remainder of the oil and vinegar. This is dressing enough for a salad for six persons. If you like the flavor of onion, grate a little juice into the dressing. The juice is obtained by first peeling the onion, and then grating with a coarse grater, using a good deal of pressure. Two strokes will give about two drops of juice-enough for this receipe.

GASPACHO - A SPANISH BREAD SALAD

FRENCH LEGATION STATE HISTORIC SITE

Historical Note:

Recipe adapted from ***The Virginia Housewife****, Mary Randolph, 1824.*

INGREDIENTS:

1 loaf white bread, preferable sourdough, sliced
5-6 tomatoes, sliced thinly
2 English cucumbers, sliced thinly
Salt
Black pepper
1 large or 2 small onions, peeled and chopped
1 C. tomato juice
½ tsp. dry mustard
2 T. olive oil
¼ C. water

PROCESS:

Lightly toast the slices of bread. Place slices of the bread to cover the bottom of a serving bowl. Put a layer of sliced tomatoes over the bread, then a layer of sliced cucumbers. Sprinkle with salt and pepper, and chopped onion. Continue to layer in the same way until the bowl is full. Mix the tomato juice with dry mustard, olive oil, and water. Mix this all well, and pour it over the layered salad. Cover and place in the refrigerator. Make it 1-2 hours before serving.

GURKIN SALAT (CUCUMBER SALAD)

KREISCHE BREWERY STATE HISTORIC SITE

Historical Note:

*Recipe adapted from **German Cookery**, Ella Oswald, 1906.*

INGREDIENTS:

2 lbs. cucumbers
A pinch of salt
1 tsp. of sugar
4 T. vinegar
1 tsp. black pepper
1 T. chopped parsley

PROCESS:

Wash the cucumbers and slice very thinly, sprinkle with salt and sugar. Stir to coat the cucumber slices. Add the vinegar to the bowl, mix well. Sprinkle the black pepper and parsley over the top. Salad oil may be added is desired, or 4 ounces of sour cream. Lemon juice may be substituted for the vinegar.

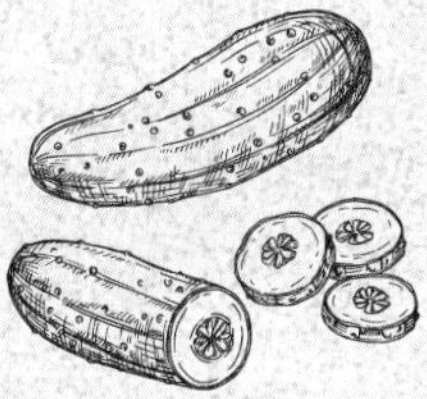

JERUSALEM ARTICHOKE SALAD

STARR FAMILY HOME STATE HISTORIC SITE

Historical Note:

*Recipe adapted from **Practical American Cookery and Household Management**, Julia Corson, 1886.*

INGREDIENTS:

Jerusalem artichokes, boiled
3 T. oil to 1 T. vinegar
1 Salt spoonful of salt (¼ tsp)
Pinch of pepper

PROCESS:

Use cold boiled artichokes; slice them without breaking them, arrange the slices neatly on a dish, and pour over them a plain salad-dressing made by mixing together three tablespoonfuls of oil to one of vinegar, a saltspoonful of salt, and pepper.

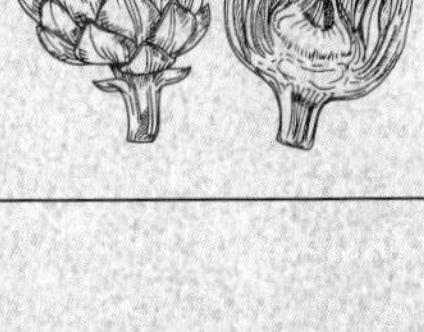

Interpreters preparing supper at Fort McKavett State Historic Site, Fort McKavett, Texas.

ORANGE SALAD

STARR FAMILY HOME
STATE HISTORIC SITE

Historical Note:

This salad is very refreshing in hot weather, and can also be made with lemons, or a combination of oranges and lemons. Recipe was adapted from ***The White House Cookbook****, 1887.*

INGREDIENTS:

4 or 5 oranges
2 T. lemon juice
5 T. salad oil
Salt
Cayenne pepper

PROCESS:

Thinly slice the oranges and place in a bowl. Mix the dressing of the lemon juice and oil. Season to taste with salt and cayenne. Pour over the sliced oranges and chill

PLAIN SALAD DRESSING

STARR FAMILY HOME
STATE HISTORIC SITE

Historical Note:

Recipe adapted from ***Practical American Cookery and Household Management****, Julia Corson,1886.*

INGREDIENTS:

6 T. oil
2 T. vinegar
1 Salt spoonful of salt (¼ tsp.)
½ salt spoonful of pepper (⅛ tsp.)
Cold string beans (optional)

PROCESS:

Mix oil, vinegar, salt, and pepper thoroughly; pour over the beans, and serve the salad. Cold string beans make a good salad.

RED VEGETABLE SALAD

STARR FAMILY HOME STATE HISTORIC SITE

Historical Note:

*Recipe adapted from **Miss Parola's New Cook Book**, Maria Parola, 1882.*

INGREDIENTS:

1 pt. of cold boiled potatoes
2 tsp. of salt (unless they were boiled in salt water)
1 pt. of cold boiled beets
Vegetables that have been cooked (1 pt. of uncooked red cabbage)
Cold string beans (optional)
6 T. oil
½ tsp. of pepper
8 T. red vinegar

PROCESS:

Cut the potatoes in thin slices and the beets fine and slice the cabbage as thin as possible. Mix together the oil, pepper, and vinegar; pour over vegetables. Let stand in a cold place one hour; then serve. Red cabbage and celery may be used together. The French dressing recipe may also be used for this recipe (page 26).

SALAD OF FRENCH BEANS

STARR FAMILY HOME STATE HISTORIC SITE

Historical Note:

*Recipe adapted from **Practical American Cookery and Household Management**, Julia Corson, 1886.*

INGREDIENTS:

1 pt. of French haricot beans
2 T. chopped parsley (the large, dark-red variety)
Water for boiling and 1 C. cold water
Plain salad-dressing
Chopped parsley

PROCESS:

Pick over a pint of French haricot beans, the large, dark-red variety; put them over the fire in a quart of cold water, and let them begin to boil; then add a cupful of cold water, and let them boil again; every fifteen minutes add more cold water, and continue to boil the beans until they are tender; then drain them, and let them get quite cold. To each pint of cold boiled beans, add two tablespoons of chopped parsley, and the plain salad-dressing. (page 31).

TOMATO ASPIC & OLIVES

STARR FAMILY HOME STATE HISTORIC SITE

Historical Note:

This recipe was originally written down by Clara Willoughby, Frank and Clara Starr's daughter. Mrs. Willoughby inherited Maplecroft, and later granted the property and furnishings to the State of Texas. The original recipe does not mention the type of mold or pan used, but usually a gelatin mold was used and the firm salad was turned out of the mold and presented on a bed of lettuce.

INGREDIENTS:

1 envelope of Knox gelatin
½ C. cold water
½ onion, cook with tomatoes
1 can of tomatoes, chopped
1 bottle of olives, sliced
Juice of one lemon
Salt to taste

PROCESS:

Soak gelatin in ¼ cup of cold water. Add onions to the canned tomatoes and bring to boiling point; strain and add to the gelatin, then add other ingredients. Pour into mold and refrigerate until firm. Invert onto bed of lettuce and serve cold.

TO KEEP TOMATAS.—Take fine ripe tomatas, and wipe them dry, taking care not to break the skin. Put them into a stone jar with cold vinegar, adding a small thin muslin bag filled with mace, whole cloves, and whole peppers. Then cork the jar tightly with a cork that has been dipped in melted rosin, and put it away in a dry place. Tomatas pickled in this manner keep perfectly well and retain their colour. For this purpose use the small round button tomatas.

Morella cherries may be pickled thus, in cold vinegar.

37*

Early Statehood
1846-1861

Texas joined the United States on December 29 of 1845 and its official transfer to statehood occurred on February 19, 1846. This transition ushered in a wave of new settlers from the United States and Europe. Among the most prominent immigrant groups were Mexicans, Germans, Czechs, French, English, and American settlers from the upper South and Midwest regions each bringing their own culinary traditions with them. Sausage-making, an important tradition from German and Czech immigrants, blended with Hispanic methods, contributing to the unique style of Texas barbecue that began to emerge during this period.

The culinary traditions of these peoples were varied, but they differed significantly from those of mainstream Americans. Anglo-Americans reported extensively on the new and unusual foods eaten by Hispanics. In San Antonio, Frederick Law Olmsted, a journalist who later became a well-known landscape architect, was served tortillas, tamales, and hashed meat (likely the precursor of chili con carne) in the 1850s. While walking through Texas during the 1850s, Stephen Powers noted "long strips of beef, and large quantities of red and green peppers and garlic." Towards the end of the 1850s Pierre Fourier Parisot reported that tortillas and frijoles were the principal foods of the Mexican ranchero sometimes supplemented with chile, eggs, and chili con carne.

The early statehood period saw an increased reliance on smoked meats, as settlers adapted their methods to the abundant livestock and the needs of a growing population. Pork remained the dominant protein, but beef also began to take hold, particularly as the cattle industry expanded. However, cattle were more valuable as dairy producers than sources of meat.

With the arrival of new settlers and the expansion of agriculture, the culinary landscape of Texas was rapidly evolving. The mixture of foods and techniques from different cultures helped create a regional cuisine that would lay the groundwork for the vibrant food culture that would define Texas in the years to come.

Chief of Interpretation, Hal Simon, conducting foodways programming at Landmark Inn State Historic Site, Castroville, Texas.

Soups and Stews

ALBONDIGAS

MAGOFFIN HOME STATE HISTORIC SITE

Historical Note:

Octavia Magoffin submitted this recipe for ***The El Paso Cook Book*** *in 1898. Albondigas is a type of meatball often made to use in soups. Mrs. Magoffin's recipe is a very simple version and can be added to with vegetables and spices.*

INGREDIENTS:

2 lbs. of Hamburg steak
4 soda crackers dissolved in liquid from tomatoes
Salt and pepper for seasoning
2 eggs
A spoonful of lard
A little chopped onion
1 can of tomatoes, liquid reserved
Water

PROCESS:

Mix well the Hamburg steak with the soda crackers, salt and pepper, and the two eggs. In a stew pan heat a spoonful of lard and put a little chopped onion and tomatoes, fry for a few moments, then fill the vessel half full of water. When coming to a boil make the meat mixture into balls, size of a partridge egg; drop into water and cook for two hours and a half.

Tia Magoffin's dining room and kitchen, Magoffin Home State Historic Site, El Paso, Texas.

BARBARA BUSH'S ZUCCHINI SOUP

BUSH FAMILY HOME
STATE HISTORIC SITE

Historical Note:

This recipe is a quick and easy soup that was a favorite in the Bush family. It was served at the George Bush Presidential Library Center's 2010 celebration in honor of the USO.

INGREDIENTS:

1 pound zucchini (about 2 large zucchini), diced
2 T. shallot (or red or white onion, whatever you have on hand)
1 clove garlic, minced
2 T. butter
1 tsp. curry powder
1¾ C. chicken broth (you can substitute beef or vegetable broth)
½ C. cream

PROCESS:

Melt butter in large frying pan over medium heat. Add diced zucchini and shallots. Cook for 8-10 minutes or until veggies soften. Add garlic and cook until fragrant. Add curry powder. Cook for another 10 minutes or until vegetables are golden brown. Pour cooked vegetables into a blender and add chicken broth and cream. Blend until smooth. Serve immediately.

"I used a little less because I was afraid the curry would overpower everything - it didn't."

–Barbara Bush

DRIED BEAN SOUP (FROM STOCK)
FORT MCKAVETT STATE HISTORIC SITE

"The bean ration was an important factor in the sustenance of the army, and no edible, I think, was so thoroughly appreciated. Company cooks stewed them with pork, and when the pork was good and the stew or soup was well done and not burned-a rare combination of circumstances,-they were quite palatable in this way."

John D. Billings, in his memoir of the Civil War.

INGREDIENTS:

2 qt. dried beans
1 gal. boiling water
2 lbs. bacon
1 gal. stock
Salt and pepper to taste

PROCESS:

Wash the beans and soak them overnight. In the morning drain the water off, and cover them again with the boiling water; add the bacon and boil gently two hours or more; now add the stock. Press the beans through a sieve, return them to the soup kettle, and bring to a boil; add salt and pepper, and serve with toasted bread.

GREEN CORN SOUP
SAM BELL MAXEY HOUSE STATE HISTORIC SITE

Historical Note:

*Recipe adapted from **The Texas Cookbook: A Thorough Treatise on the Art of Cookery, 1883**. The cookbook was published by the ladies of the First Presbyterian Church of Houston. The term "green corn" is in the name of the recipe to differentiate from dried corn.*

INGREDIENTS:

6 ears of corn on the cob
Water
1 qt. milk
Butter, salt, and pepper

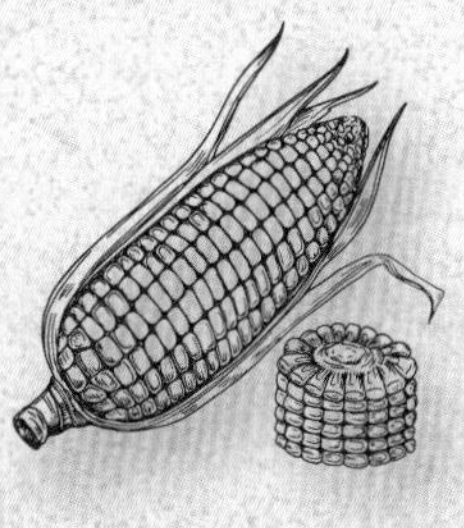

PROCESS:

Grate the corn off of the cobs. Place the cobs in a pan with enough water to cover and bring them to a boil for about 20 minutes. Remove the cobs and use the water to stew the grated corn until softened. Add the quart of milk and bring it to a slow boil. Remove if from the stove and season it with butter, salt, and pepper to taste.

GREEN TURTLE SOUP

FULTON MANSION STATE HISTORIC SITE

Historical Note:

Recipe adapted from ***What Mrs. Fisher knows about Old Southern Cooking, Soups, Pickles, Preserves, Etc.***, Abby Fisher, 1881. *Due to their abundance in the area, particularly on islands and sandbars in and around Aransas Bay, sea turtles were often hunted for their meat. The Fultons would have served turtle soup often when entertaining as it was considered a delicacy.*

INGREDIENTS:

2 lbs. turtle meat
2 qt. water
Pepper and salt to taste
3 hard-boiled eggs
¼ of a lemon
8 T. dry sherry

PROCESS:

To two pounds of turtle meat add two quarts of water and bring to a slow boil, allowing it to reduce down to three pints. Season with salt and pepper to taste. Take three hardboiled eggs, slice them very thin and lay them in the bottom of a tureen. Add three tablespoons of dry sherry. Pour the hot soup into tureen and serve. This recipe makes 20 servings.

DISCLAIMER: This recipe has been included here for historical interest only as all seven sea turtle varieties are listed and protected under the U.S. Endangered Species Act. The hunting or possession of any portion of a sea turtle carries a maximum federal fine of $25,000.

Fulton Mansion State Historic Site, Fulton, Texas.

KARTOFFEL SUPPE (POTATO SOUP)

KREISCHE BREWERY STATE HISTORIC SITE

Historical Note:

Recipe adapted from ***German Cookery****, Ella Oswald, 1906.*

INGREDIENTS:

4 oz. butter
1 lb. potatoes, finely chopped
1 small head celery, finely chopped
1 onion finely chopped
A pinch of allspice
A few ground peppercorns
Dried savory herbs
1 oz. flour
1 qt. water
1 C. beef broth
1 tsp. chopped parsley

PROCESS:

Melt the butter in a very hot saucepan and then add all of the vegetables. Mix the allspice, black pepper, and herbs with the flour and add them to the pan. Add the water and beef broth. Boil until the vegetables are very soft. Pass everything through a sieve, pressing the cooked vegetable through too. Garnish with chopped parsley and serve with toasted bread.

ONION SOUP

LANDMARK INN STATE HISTORIC SITE

Historical Note:

Recipe adapted from ***The Virginia Housewife,*** *Mary Randolph,1824.*

INGREDIENTS:

10 onions
1 C. butter
2 T. flour
4 C. boiling water or beef stock
1 large slice of bread
Salt and pepper to taste
1 egg yolk
1 tsp. vinegar

PROCESS:

Peel and chop the onions. Melt the butter in a large stew pot or Dutch oven and add the onions. Cook until they are browned but not caramelized. Add the flour and stir well to blend. Add the water or stock to the pot. Lay a slice of bread on top of the mixture, and add salt and pepper to taste. Stew for 15 to 20 minutes. Beat one egg yolk with vinegar. Add a small amount of the hot stock to the egg yolk mixture in a small bowl to temper the egg. Pour the egg, vinegar, and broth mixture into the pot and stir to gradually thicken. Served with toasted bread.

PORK STEW WITH VEGETABLES
FORT MARTIN SCOTT STATE HISTORIC SITE

Historical Note:

Recipe adapted from ***Culinary Hints for the Soldier****, Capt. James M. Sanderson, 1862. Dehydrated (or as they were called in the 19th century "Desiccated") vegetables were commercially available by the mid-19th century and used by the military and settlers as an easy way to carry large amounts of food over greater distances and it would keep longer in dry situations.*

INGREDIENTS:

1 gallon of water
1 4-lb. boneless pork roast
2 T. lard or shortening
2 C. mixed dehydrated vegetables (usually premixed carrots, onion, peas, celery, peppers, green beans, and parsley)
Salt and pepper to taste
3 T. vinegar
½ loaf of stale/toasted bread (optional)

PROCESS:

Put the water into a large stew pot and bring to a boil. Cut the pork into pieces about 1 inch square. Add the lard or shortening to a pan and heat until it is melted and sizzling. Add the pork cubes and cook in batches allowing them to become well browned. Place the browned pork cubes and dehydrated vegetables into the boiling water and reduce the heat to a gentle boil for an hour and one half. Season with salt pepper and the vinegar. If there is stale or toasted bread available quarter each slice and add it to the soup and stir it in. Cook for a further 15 minutes at a slow boil and until the soup is somewhat thickened.

French Legation State Historic Site, Austin, Texas.

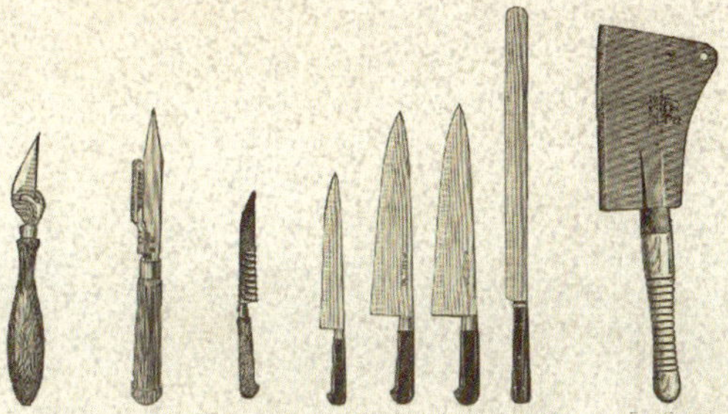

POSOLE

FORT LANCASTER STATE HISTORIC SITE

Historical Note:

Posole, which originated in Aztec culture in central Mexico where it was used in religious ceremonies, became a staple in the foodways of Southwestern America by the mid-19th century. It is a hearty stew based around hominy. To create hominy, corn is dried on the cob, removed, and soaked in a lye and water solution to cause the kernel to swell and split the hard skin on their exterior. It is then preserved by either drying or canning for later use.

INGREDIENTS:

2 white onions, diced
3 lbs. pork, cubed
2 25 oz. cans of hominy
1 bay leaf
2 cloves garlic, minced
1 tsp. salt (more to taste)
½ tsp pepper
4-5 C. chicken broth
14 oz. puréed red or green chili
Enchilada sauce
½ tsp. oregano
¼ tsp cumin

PROCESS:

Sauté onions and pork then add all other ingredients. Cook until pork is tender. (You can do it in a slow cooker for 4 to 6 hours.)

SPLIT PEA STEW WITH BEEF (KNOWN AS THE "GREEN DEATH")

MISSION DOLORES STATE HISTORIC SITE

Historical Note:

Recipes like this were utilized by the friars and soldiers living at Mission Dolores, having been introduced to them by French traders from the nearby Fort St. Jean Baptiste in French Louisiana. Its simplicity and ability to provide a filling meal made it particularly valuable. Recipe is from the Fort St. Jean Baptiste Louisiana State Historic Site, Foodways Program.

INGREDIENTS:

½ lb. dried peas (soak overnight)
½ lb. beef
Flour (for coating beef)
3 pt. boiling water
Potatoes, cubed
Onions, chopped
Parsnips, chopped
Salt and pepper to taste

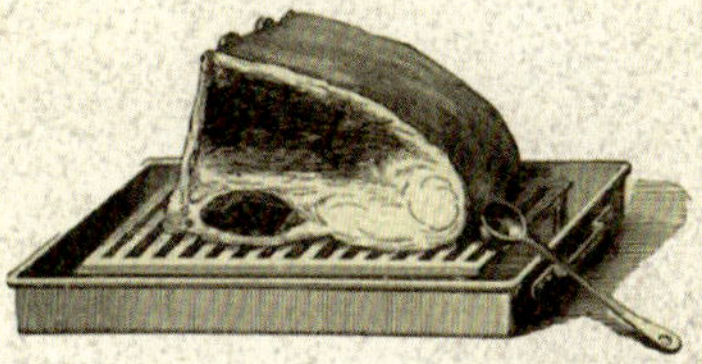

PROCESS:

Soak dried peas overnight so they are ready to cook. Drain before adding to stew. Start out with half a pound of beef. Coating the meat with flour and then browning it will help thicken up the stew. While browning the beef, bring water to a boil. Add beef and peas, boiling for 15 minutes. Once stew has boiled for 15 minutes, add potatoes, onion, parsnips, salt, and pepper. The amount of these items to add is left up to the cook's preference and taste. This will need to simmer for an hour. The stew is ready when the peas break down and stew thickens up. The humorous nickname "The Green Death" arose due to the stew's distinctive appearance and robust flavors, which varied depending on the cook's preparation.

TJ GREEN & COMPANY STEW

MONUMENT HILL STATE HISTORIC SITE

Historical Note:

While imprisoned in Perote Prison in Mexico, Thomas Jefferson Green and fellow prisoners cooked this stew, and it was declared, "The very best dish we had cooked."

INGREDIENTS:

½ lb. stew beef
2 T. lard, divided
¾ medium yellow onion, diced
2 cloves garlic, minced*
2 New Mexico red chiles, re-hydrated and minced
1 tomato, diced*
½ tsp. Mexican oregano*
3 small red potatoes, peeled and cut in ½ inch chunks
2 C. water
¼ C. milk (to be authentic, use donkey milk)
Salt to taste

**Since not specified, you may determine which "condiments" to include based on personal taste.*

PROCESS:

Brown the beef in about 1 tablespoon of lard over medium heat. Remove beef from pot. Add the remaining tablespoon of lard to the pot. Add onions and cook until translucent, about 10 minutes. Add garlic and cook for another 1-2 minutes. Stir in chiles, diced tomatoes, and oregano. Add potatoes and return beef to the pot. Add water and milk. Bring to boil; reduce heat and simmer until beef is tender, about 1 hour. Season with salt to taste and add water/milk as necessary to maintain adequate broth. For serving, individual bowls can be garnished with sliced jalapeños, diced onion, and chopped cilantro.

Site Manager, Cody Mobley, conducting foodways programming at Fort McKavett State Historic Site, Fort McKavett, Texas.

TO MAKE AN OLLO, A SPANISH DISH
LANDMARK INN
STATE HISTORIC SITE

Historical Note:

Recipe adapted from ***The Virginia Housewife****, Mary Randolph, 1824.*

INGREDIENTS:

2 lbs. beef roast
1 lb. lamb roast or 2 lamb shanks
One chicken, quartered
1 small piece of salt pork
2 onions, chopped small
Salt and pepper to taste
4 C. water
3 apples or pears, peeled and cut in two
3 tomatoes with the skins removed
3 C. green beans, snapped
½ C. mint leaves, chopped
1 bunch celery, diced

PROCESS:

Place the beef, lamb, quartered chicken, and salt pork in a pot with the chopped onion, salt, and pepper. Add three to four cups of water. Cover and gently let it stew for two hours. Add the cut apples or pears, tomatoes, green beans, and mint. Adjust the amount of water as necessary so that it does not cook dry. Gently let it stew for two more hours. Add the celery, adjusting the amount of water if necessary and let it stew for one hour more.

Smokehouse at Barrington Living History Farm State Historic Site, Washington, Texas.

EARLY MODERN ERA
1868-1890

The end of the Civil War and the growth of the cattle industry helped shape the culinary identity of late 19th-century Texas. With the expansion of cattle ranching, beef became the primary protein in Texas kitchens, and new dishes, such as steaks, stews, and chile con carne, emerged. These dishes reflected a fusion of American and Mexican culinary traditions, with chili peppers and other indigenous ingredients dominating the flavor profile.

The railroad's arrival also played a key role in shaping the foodways of the time by facilitating the transport of goods and people. The advent of refrigerated rail cars made it possible to ship frozen beef across the state and country. Even items like fresh oysters shipped in barrels of sea water became common. This made it easier to move food supplies across the state and beyond, allowing for the exchange of culinary ideas.

The popularity of Texas-style barbecue, particularly beef brisket, became a defining feature of the state's cuisine, setting it apart from other regional barbecue traditions. Some of today's oldest barbecue restaurants have their roots in meat markets established in the 1880s.

From Pen to Pastry: The Story of Eliza Leslie

Eliza Leslie was born in Philadelphia, Pennsylvania, in 1787, the eldest of five children. At age five, she moved with her family to England, where her father pursued a clockmaking export business. A gifted man, he nurtured Eliza's love for reading, writing, and drawing. She began writing poetry early, though she became discouraged and gradually abandoned hopes of being published. After her father's death in 1803, the family faced financial hardship, and she and her mother supported themselves by taking in boarders.

In the 1820s, Eliza attended Mrs. Goodfellow's cooking school in Philadelphia. Sharing the recipes with friends inspired her first book, ***Seventy-Five Receipts for Pastry, Cakes, and Sweetmeats***, 1828, which was a success.

Eliza Leslie became one of the most prolific authors of the 19th century. In addition to fiction and nonfiction, Eliza, often called Miss Leslie, became most noted for her cookbooks. Her book ***Directions for Cookery, in its Various Branches,*** 1837, became the century's best-selling cookbook, with over 150,000 copies sold. Her more specialized ***Domestic French Cookery***, 1836, was highly influential and regarded as introducing French cuisine to a broad American audience.

Entrées and Main Dishes

FLAMMEKUECHE, AN ALSATIAN ONION PIE

LANDMARK INN STATE HISTORIC SITE

Historical Note:

This traditional recipe is from Katelyn Haegelin and Kerri Zinsmeyer, owners of the All Local – Market in Castroville, Texas. It is a recipe handed down within Alsatian families for many years.

INGREDIENTS:

6 oz. bacon, thinly sliced crosswise
4 C. yellow onion, thinly sliced
8 oz crème fraîche
1 large egg yolk
Pinch nutmeg
Kosher salt and ground black pepper to taste
1 ½ lb. ball purchased pizza dough, room temperature
3 oz. coarsely grated Gruyere cheese
Parchment paper

NOTE: You will need three sheets of kitchen parchment for use on the baking sheets.

PROCESS:

In a large skillet over medium heat, cook the bacon, stirring until it starts to brown, 5 to 8 minutes. Transfer the bacon to paper towels to drain and pour off all but 2 tablespoons of the fat from the skillet. Return the skillet to medium heat and add the onion. Cook, covered, stirring occasionally, until very soft, about 10 minutes. Remove the cover and cook, stirring occasionally, until golden brown, about another 30 minutes. Season with salt and pepper, then set aside.

Heat the oven to 500 degrees. Arrange one of the oven racks on the oven's bottom shelf. In a small bowl, stir together the crème fraîche, egg yolk, nutmeg, and a pinch of salt and pepper. Divide the dough into three even pieces. On a lightly oiled surface, roll out each piece into a 10 by 12 inch rectangle about 1/8 inch thick. Transfer each to a 15 x 17 inch sheet of kitchen parchment. The dough may shrink and lose its shape. If so, roll it again on the parchment. One at a time, transfer each piece of parchment and dough to baking sheet.

Spread a third of the crème fraîche mixture over one piece of dough on a baking sheet, top with one third of the onions and bacon. Sprinkle with one third of the cheese. Bake on the oven's lower rack for 10 minutes, or until the crust is crisp. Repeat with remaining dough and toppings. Serve right away. Makes three 10 to 12 inch flat pies.

BAKED TONGUE

FRENCH LEGATION STATE HISTORIC SITE

Historical Note:

*Recipe adapted from **Domestic French Cookery, Chiefly Translated from Sulpice Barué**, Miss Eliza Leslie, 1836. This was the first French cookbook translated for the American market.*

INGREDIENTS:

A sliced cold boiled beef tongue
Vinegar
Capers
Parsley, finely minced
Shallots, finely minced
Grated bread
Warm water

PROCESS:

Take a cold boiled tongue and cut it into slices; set aside. Put in the bottom of a deep dish a little vinegar, with the capers, parsley, shallots, and some grated bread, all mixed together. Lay the slices of tongue upon this and cover them with some more of the same seasoning. Then grate some bread all over the top. Moisten the whole by pouring in a little warm water. Put the dish into a stove moderately heated. Bake it until brown.

BARBECUED WIENERS

STARR FAMILY HOME STATE HISTORIC SITE

Historical Note:

In the notes for the original recipe, Miss Clara Starr mentions that she "usually put more of the chopped vegetables--abo a cup of each because I like thick sauce".

INGREDIENTS:

1 T. white sugar
1½ T. brown sugar
¼ tsp. salt
1 T. flour
2½ tsp. vinegar
1¼ C. water
⅔ C. catsup
1 tsp. Worcestershire
⅓ C. onions, chopped
½ C. carrots, chopped
¼ C. celery, chopped
¼ C. celery leaves, chopped
⅛ tsp. garlic, minced fine
1½ lbs. wieners

PROCESS:

Mix dry ingredients and add liquids and chopped vegetables. Put wieners in baking pan and pour the sauce mixture over them. Cook covered in oven at 350° for 2 to 2 ½ hours.

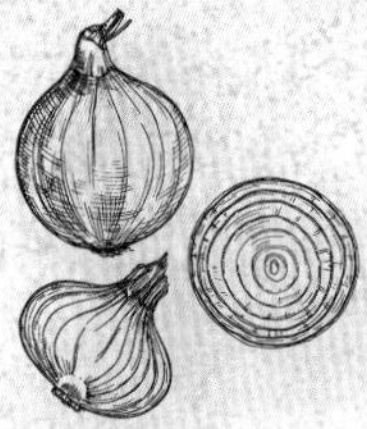

BOUDIN

SAN JACINTO BATTLEGROUND STATE HISTORIC SITE

Historical Note:

This recipe is from Mary Jane Harris Briscoe who was the wife of Andrew Briscoe. He was a signer of the Texas Declaration of Independence and fought at the Battle of San Jacinto.

INGREDIENTS:

1 T. butter
2 T. dry breadcrumbs
½ C. water or stock
Salt and pepper to taste
1 pre-c meat (precut meat)
3 eggs, well beaten
1 T. salt
1 T. parsley

PROCESS:

Place butter, crumbs, and water or stock over fire. Add the seasonings to the meat. Mix together. Stir in carefully the 3 eggs, well beaten until well done. This may be fried in small patties as fresh sausage or stuffed into casings for boiling.

42 *Sausage Meat Cutter.*—Will cut four pounds of meat per minute for sausages hash, &c

uaker stove at Starr Family Home State Historic Site, Marshall, Texas.

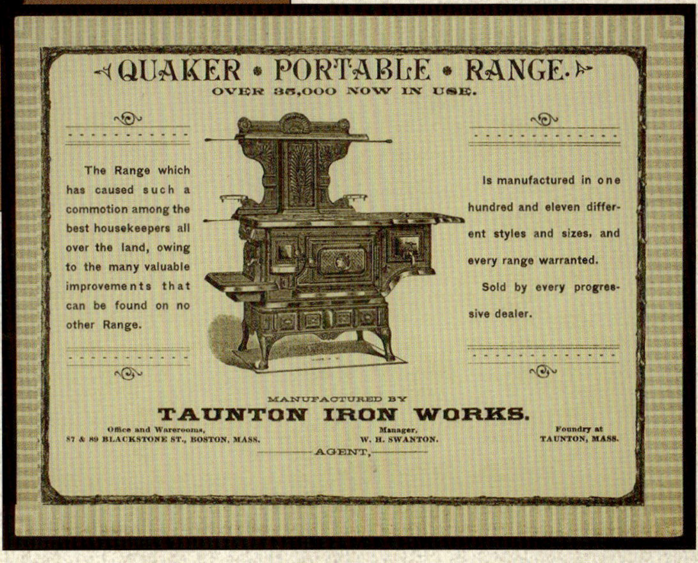

BUFFALO (OR BEEF) STEAKS
CHARLES AND MARY ANN GOODNIGHT RANCH STATE HISTORIC SITE

Historical Note:

This was an easy and quick meal "Cookie," the cook of the chuckwagon, would make for cowboys after a long day of driving cattle on the frontier. This recipe is adapted from ***Legends of America, Traveling through American History, Destination, and Legends.***

INGREDIENTS:

3 tsp. ground coffee
3 tsp. ground chipotle pepper or powder
¼ cup paprika
2 tsp. toasted cumin seeds
3 T. sugar
1 T. salt
4 buffalo or beef steaks (8 oz. each)

PROCESS:

Combine coffee, ground chipotle, paprika, cumin seeds, sugar, and salt. Rub the mixture into steaks. Grill steaks until desired doneness. Makes four servings.

Charles Goodnight is credited with inventing the chuckwagon in 1866. One of the most prominent cattlemen of his time, he wanted to ensure that his cowboys were fed on long cattle drives. He made modifications to a Studebaker Army wagon to create a mobile kitchen. This invention changed the cattle industry by allowing cowboys to carry enough food and supplies to drive cattle for weeks.

1917 chuckwagon on display at the Charles and Mary Ann Goodnight Ranch State Historic Site, Clarendon, Texas.

CHICKEN DUMPLINGS

CONFEDERATE REUNION GROUNDS STATE HISTORIC SITE

Historical Note:

Recipe adapted from ***Dr. Price's Cream Baking Powder Cookbook, 1916.***

INGREDIENTS:

1 cold boiled chicken
½ C. chicken broth
Sage, rosemary, parsley to taste
1 T. flour
Little cold water
3 egg yolks
1 whole egg
½ C. milk
Bread or cracker crumbs
Lard or shortening

PROCESS:

De-bone a cold boiled chicken and mince the meat and place it in a sauce pan with ½ cup chicken broth and minced sage, rosemary, and parsley to taste. Heat to a gentle boil. Wet one tablespoon of flour with a little cold water and add it to the pan. Beat three egg yolks together and add them to the pan. Stir constantly until it thickens. Pour out onto a rimmed baking pan, cover, and chill in refrigerator.

Once cold remove the chicken mixture from the refrigerator, flour your hands, and roll mixture into 1 to 1-1/2 inch balls. Roll the balls in the bread or cracker crumbs. Mix a thin batter of one-half cup milk and flour, roll meatballs in batter and then again in bread or cracker crumbs. Fry them in hot lard or shortening.

CHILE CON CARNE

MAGOFFIN HOME STATE HISTORIC SITE

Historical Note:

*This Tex-Mex dish seemes to have been very popular in the late 1800s as **The El Paso Cook Book** published several submissions of this recipe. This recipe belonged to Octavia Magoffin. It must have been a hit to the many guests who stayed in the home during those formative years of El Paso.*

INGREDIENTS:

1 steak cut into small pieces
One good sized onion, cut up
Some tomatoes, cut up
Spoonful of lard
12 large dry red peppers
1 T. vinegar
Salt to taste

PROCESS:

Take a nice steak cut into small pieces; cut up a good sized onion and some tomatoes; take a stew pan, heat with spoon of lard, put in the meat and cover--into another vessel put twelve large dry red peppers, after washing and removing seed; cover with water and boil until soft; put in a strainer and with potato masher rub well; pour this mixture into the meat; add one tablespoon of vinegar, salt to taste. Cook two and a half hours.

CROQUETTES

SAN JACINTO BATTLEGROUND STATE HISTORIC SITE

Historical Note:

This recipe is also from the collection of recipes belonging to Mary Jane Harris Briscoe. She was active in the Texas Veterans Association and the founder and first president of Sheltering Arms, a home for needy women in Houston. She wrote sketches and reminiscences and was a charter member and honorary life member of the Texas State Historical Association.

INGREDIENTS:

1 pt. cold meat cut fine
1 T. chopped parsley
¼ tsp. nutmeg, grated
Salt and pepper to taste
1 tsp. onion juice
½ pt. milk
1 oz. or 1 T. butter
2 T. of flour

PROCESS:

Add seasonings together with the meat. Put milk over the fire. Rub butter and flour together and add to the milk. Stir until thickened, mix in the meat. Shape into patties and fry in a skillet.

ECONOMY LOAF

NATIONAL MUSEUM OF THE PACIFIC WAR STATE HISTORIC SITE

Historical Note:

This recipe is from a collection of recipes taken from ***Recipes For Today****, published by the General Foods Corporation, 1943.*

INGREDIENTS:

6 T. vitaminized margarine
½ C. dry breadcrumbs
1 C. cooked fresh or canned peas
1 C. mashed potatoes
¼ tsp. salt
⅛ tsp. pepper
⅛ tsp. nutmeg
2 T. flour
½ C. milk
2 hard-boiled eggs
1 can condensed tomato soup
Additional seasonings

PROCESS:

Melt 2 tablespoons of margarine in a saucepan, add crumbs, brown slightly, stirring constantly. Sprinkle half the crumbs on the bottom and sides of a well greased oblong loaf pan (approximately 8½ x 4½ x 2¾ inches). Mash peas through a sieve, add mashed potatoes, remaining crumbs and seasonings. Make white sauce by melting 2 tablespoons of the margarine, adding flour, then the milk, cooking until smooth and thickened. Add white sauce to potato mixture, blend together thoroughly. Place half of this mixture in crumb lined loaf pan. Top with slices of hard-boiled egg; add remaining potato mixture. Bake in moderate oven (350 degrees) for 25 minutes or until set. Unmold, garnish with additional egg slices, or with broiled bacon, if desired. Serve with tomato sauce made by heating the soup with the remaining 2 tablespoons margarine, adding a pinch of herbs and a little Worchestershire or A-1 Sauce, to taste.

FLOUNDERS BROILED
SABINE PASS STATE HISTORIC SITE

Historical Note:

*Located on the Sabine River not very far inland from the Gulf, the Sabine Pass area has historically been a prime fishing spot for flounder. Without a doubt the Confederate soldier's station at the Sabine Pass fortifications would have supplemented their army diet with fresh fish from the waters of the Pass. Recipe adapted from **Every Lady's Cook Book**, Mrs. T. J. Crowen,1856. The flounder in this recipe would have originally been cooked on a gridiron, which resembled a barbecue grill with legs so that it could be placed over live coals to cook. The bottom side of the fish would cook before being flipped to cook the opposite side.*

INGREDIENTS:

1 whole flounder per person, gutted and cleaned with the scales scraped off
Salt and pepper
1½ C. flour
1 T. bacon drippings or lard

PROCESS:

Wash the fish and scrape them clean inside and out. Dry them with a cloth, and season them inside with a little salt and pepper to taste. Dredge them in flour. Grease a broiler pan with the drippings or lard and lay the fish on it. Place under oven broiler until each side turns golden and crispy, turning halfway through cooking. Once done, lay them on a serving platter and add salt and pepper to taste to the outside.

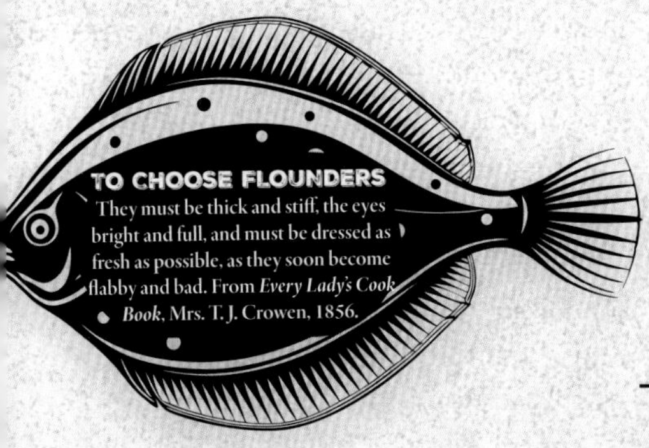

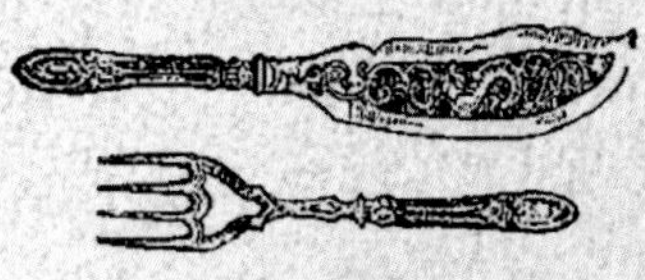

FISH CARVERS.

FRIED FLOUNDERS
SABINE PASS STATE HISTORIC SITE

Historical Note:

*Recipe adapted from **Mrs. Beeton's Book of Household Management**, Isabella Beeton, 1861. Mrs. Beeton states that flounder was in season August through November and were an economical fish to serve*

INGREDIENTS:

1 flounder per person
Salt
2-3 eggs
2 C. breadcrumbs
Enough lard in which to fry the whole fish
Parsley

PROCESS:

Clean the fish. Two hours before you intend to cook them, rub them inside and out with salt to render them firm. Wash and wipe them very dry. Whisk the eggs together until frothy and dip each flounder into the eggs. Dredge them in breadcrumbs. Fry them in boiling lard, 5 to 10 minutes depending on their size. Place them on a towel or napkin to drain, then plate them and garnish with crisped flash-fried parsley.

FRICASSEED CHICKEN
BARRINGTON LIVING HISTORY FARM STATE HISTORIC SITE

Historical Note:

This recipe was adapted from ***What Mrs. Fisher knows about Old Southern Cooking, Soups, Pickles, Preserves, Etc.****, Abby Fisher, 1881. Mrs. Fisher was a formerly enslaved woman who had lived in the Carolinas and Louisiana, places Dr. Jones was fond of living. Recipes like this one are a fair representation of those that might have been cooked for the Jones family.*

INGREDIENTS:

1 chicken, tender, and well cleaned inside
2 eggs, hard boiled
1 T. butter
1 T. corn starch dissolved into small bit of water
Salt and pepper to taste

PROCESS:

Chicken must be tender and well cleaned inside. Have your chicken cut up before boiling. Singe all pin feathers off over the fire. Boil two eggs hard, take the yolks and rub fine into one tablespoon of butter, then add one tablespoon of corn starch dissolved into the least bit of water; add all together, well mixed and free from lumps. Have your chicken cut up before boiling. Stir the fricassee into the boiling chicken just before sending to table. Season with salt and pepper while cooking.

Fricasseed Chicken before being added to the stew. Barrington Living History Farm, Washington, Texas.

HAMBURGER PIE
SAM RAYBURN HOUSE STATE HISTORIC SITE

Historical Note:

Meatloaf, chilis, and hamburger pies, like this recipe were very popular in the 1930s. This recipe is adapted from ***Fannin County Home Demonstration Club Cookbook*** *by Mrs. C. L. Melugin and is a great example of the simplistic style of home cooking, that often incorporated canned vegetables.*

INGREDIENTS:

2 lbs. ground meat
small amount of lard
1 No. 2 can of tomatoes
1 medium-sized onion, cut fine
Salt and pepper to taste
½ C. corn meal with enough water to make a mush
1 lump of lard the size of an egg

PROCESS:

Cook 2 lb. hamburger meat in a little lard until it turns light and crumbles apart. Mix with one No. 2 can of tomatoes. Cut 1 medium-sized onion fine, add salt and black pepper to suit taste and mix well; set aside. Make a mush with ½ cup of corn meal. Place half of meat mixture in a saucepan, add layer of mush and rest of meat mixture. Place a lump of lard the size of an egg on top and bake. We would suggest baking for 30 to 45 minutes in a 350 degree oven.

BUTCHERING AND CURING

William Oliver wrote in 1843;

"There is perhaps no animal which the western farmer possesses, reared with so little trouble and expense, and which, at the same time, adds so largely to his comforts, as the hog."

The winter months of December and January marked the time for a ritual once commonplace amongst rural Texans. "Hog killing time," as it was commonly referred to, was when farms and plantations alike began the process of butchering and curing their annual meat supply. In December 1848, Dr. Anson Jones noted in his diary that the weather had turned "severely cold...with snow and ice." A few days later he wrote "Killed 5 hogs." The enslaved at Barrington butchered a total of 10 hogs during that December cold snap.

Prior to refrigeration, the only way to preserve large quantities of meat was through a process that utilized combinations of salt, sugar, spices, and smoke. The fresh pork generally required several weeks of being packed in salt to be effectively preserved. Taking advantage of cold weather helped keep meat from spoiling while it cured.

Barrington Living History Farm continues this ritual each winter using the same methods of butchering and curing along with the same types of "unimproved" hogs raised in the 1850s. The Ossabaw Island Hog is a heritage breed that descended from the pigs brought to the Americas by Spanish explorers in the 1500s. Early farmers did little to improve specific breeds or characteristics, in fact many preferred the characteristics offered by unimproved breeds. While not native, Ossabaw hogs are a rare survivor in America and possess a unique link to our agricultural past.

Barrington is one of only a few historic farm museums in the United States that continues to breed and use these rare hogs.

PORK.

1. Leg of Pork, or Ham of Bacon.
2. Loin.
3. Thin Rib.
4. Spare Rib.
5. Hand or Shoulder.
6. Middling.
7. Chop, cheek or jowl.

ITALIAN SPAGHETTI

NATIONAL MUSEUM OF THE PACIFIC WAR STATE HISTORIC SITE

Historical Note:

Recipe from Robert Pennell, a Captain in the US Army in the Philippines, who served in the 3rd Battalion, 21st Infantry Regiment, Philippine Scouts, during the attack on Bataan on the Philippine Islands. He received a Silver Star for his actions during the defense of Bataan. Recipes are from diaries kept by Pennell while he was in the Zentsuji Prisoner-of-War Camp.

INGREDIENTS:

¼ lb. dried mushrooms
¾ lb. ground round beef
¼ lb. ground lean pork
Little bit of chopped onion
2 cloves of garlic, ground fine
Salt and pepper
Breadcrumbs
1 T. chopped parsley
Tabasco Sauce
1 egg
Juice of 1 lemon
⅕ tsp. sage
Olive oil

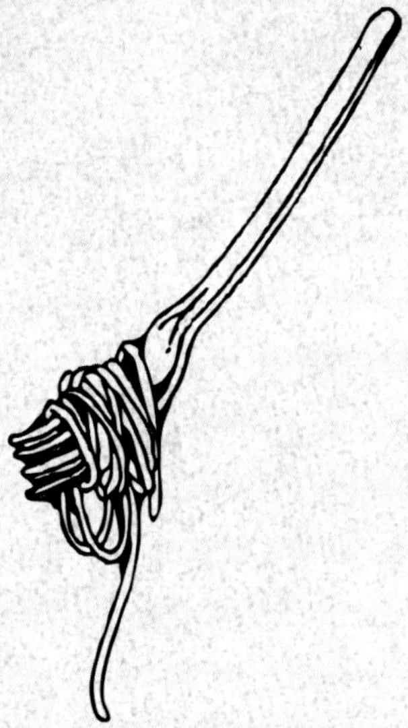

4 large onions
2 cloves garlic, finely minced
Salt and pepper
Paprika
1 can tomato soup stock
Reserved mushroom broth
½ C. red wine
Coriander
Cayenne pepper
Bouquet garni
2 Jiggers of brandy or sherry (one jigger equals 1½ oz.)
3 bundles of dry spaghetti
Grated parmesan cheese

PROCESS:

Pre-preparation: The night before, place dried mushrooms in lukewarm water and soak overnight. The next day, strain mushrooms, reserving water (mushroom broth) for use later in recipe.

Meat for sauce: Mix together ground beef and ground pork. Add a little onion, garlic, salt, pepper, a few breadcrumbs, parsley, and Tabasco Sauce. Bind with one egg, lemon juice, and sage. Dampen with hot water and form into balls. Sear meatballs in hot olive oil in an iron pot. Remove meatballs from pan; set aside. Save pan gravy.

Sauce: Finely chop rehydrated mushrooms; set aside. Chop four onions and garlic; fry onion and garlic in reserved pan gravy (pan in which meatballs were cooked) until onions start to turn golden. Add mushrooms and season with salt, pepper, and paprika. Fry for 10 minutes more. Do not permit onion to become crisp. Use plenty of oil, a low fire, and a heavy saucepan with a cover. Now add tomato paste and tomato soup; cook for one minute. Stir in coriander, cayenne pepper, and bouquet garni.

Place mixture in a casserole dish in the oven and bake at 250 degrees, adding stock as necessary, for 2 to 5 hours. Then pour mixture over seared meatballs in an iron pot and simmer on top of the stove for 45 to 60 minutes. Ten minutes before serving, add brandy or sherry. Thicken if necessary.

Spaghetti: Place dry spaghetti in a large pot of violently boiling salted water a little at a time, so as not to stop boiling. Boil until spaghetti is almost done but still slightly tough. Remove the pot from heat. Remove spaghetti from the hot water and wash in cold water. Put the rinsed spaghetti back into the hot water in pot and steam hot. Do not overcook.

To Serve: Place a layer of spaghetti on a large platter and cover with a layer of sauce and meatballs. Add a thick coating of grated Parmesan cheese. Put the remainder of the sauce in a hot casserole dish and place it on the table. Have plenty of grated cheese on the table. Serve with a light green salad.

Open hearth cooking at French Legation State Historic Site, Austin, Texas.

OPOSSUM WITH DRESSING

CONFEDERATE REUNION GROUNDS STATE HISTORIC SITE

Historical Note:

Recipe adapted from ***The Mentha-Col Successful Cooking Recipes for Simple Dishes in use by Southern Housewives****, 1921.*

INGREDIENTS:

1 cleaned and dressed opossum
5 large sweet potatoes divided
1 large onion
1 tablespoon butter
Salt and pepper to taste

PROCESS:

Boil the opossum until tender with three peeled sweet potatoes. Chop one onion very fine. Thoroughly mash the boiled sweet potatoes and mix in the chopped onion. Salt and pepper to taste. Stuff the opossum with the mashed sweet potato mix. Peel and cube the two remaining sweet potatoes into 1-inch cubes. Place the opossum in a roasting pan and surround it with the cubed sweet potatoes. Bake in a 400-degree oven for 25 minutes. Remove and place opossum on a platter surrounded by the cubed sweet potatoes and reserve the pot licker for gravy.

PANCHO'S FAMOUS SHRIMP RANCHERO

PORT ISABEL LIGHTHOUSE STATE HISTORIC SITE

Historical Note:

Pancho's Shrimp Ranchero recipe takes the best of both worlds with a seafood base and a Tex-Mex spicy flare. Pancho's father owned a restaurant where he learned and honed his craft and this recipe.

INGREDIENTS:

1 T. cooking oil
1 large tomato, quartered
1 small onion, cut lengthwise in thin strips
3 fresh jalapeños, quartered lengthwise
1 can tomatoes, cut lengthwise in thin strips
6 C. water
1 tsp. comino powder (cumin)
Salt and pepper to taste
1 lb. Gulf wild-caught shrimp, 26-30 count, peeled and de-veined
½ C. fresh cilantro, chopped

PROCESS:

In a large skillet or Dutch oven, sauté in oil fresh tomato, onion, and jalapeños. When tender add the can of tomatoes, water, and spices. Allow to boil on medium-high heat for 15 minutes. Add shrimp and cilantro. Lower heat to medium and simmer 10 minutes. Serve with Spanish rice and hot tortillas.

ROAST BEEF
FORT MCKAVETT STATE HISTORIC SITE

"The monthly expenditures in [the Fort McKavett Commissary of Subsistence] Department average $400, and are made for purchases of fresh beef and commutation of the whiskey ration of extra duty men. Beef is issued six days in every ten. The contract price is 4-9/10 cents per pound."

Brevet Lieutenant Colonel William Grigsby Freeman, Army Inspector General, August 1853.

INGREDIENTS:

5 lbs. beef round
1 lb. bacon strips
1 clove garlic
Rosemary leaves
Salt and Pepper
1 lb. lard
Half pound butter

PROCESS:

Lard the beef with bacon strips and stud with crushed garlic cloves and rosemary leaves all over. Season lightly with salt and pepper. Spit the roast and place in reflector oven no less than 18 inches from the fire. The fire must extend at least four inches past the sides of the oven. Once meat is hot, baste regularly with good sweet lard and its own drippings when produced. When the roast is nearly done, baste with good fresh butter. Roast is finished when drippings are completely clear without blood. Use drippings to make good gravy.

SAUERBRATEN

KREISCHE BREWERY STATE HISTORIC SITE

Historical Note:

Recipe adapted from ***The Encyclopedia of Practical Cookery****, Theodore Francis Garrett, 1898. Literal translation means "sour roast." It is one of the national dishes of Germany.*

INGREDIENTS:

3-4 lb. beef chuck roast
2 C. vinegar
6 strips fatty bacon
Cloves, salt, and pepper
3 T. butter
2 C. flour
3-4 carrots
1 large onion
2 bay leaves
1 lemon, zested
12-15 peppercorns
1 tsp. blade mace
Salt to taste
2 C. cold water

Stove located at the Kreische house at Kreische Brewery State Historic Site, La Grange, Texas.

PROCESS:

Place one 3 to 4 pound chuck roast into a shallow dish and cover with 2 cups of vinegar. Leave it for two to three days, turning it occasionally and basting it with the vinegar so that each part may be equally soaked. When ready to cook the meat, drain it from the vinegar and dry it with a clean cloth.

Cut 6 strips of fatty bacon to about 1-1/2 inches long. Season them well with a mix of ground cloves, salt, and pepper. With a large skewer or thin knife blade make holes in the roast and insert the pieces of spiced bacon into them, making sure to do all sides of the roast. In a Dutch oven or roasting pan large enough to hold the roast melt 3 tablespoons of butter. Dredge the roast in flour and put the roast in the pan with the butter. Turn the roast as each side becomes brown.

Peel and cut 3 to 4 carrots into quarters; peel and quarter the large onion and place them around the roast in the pan. Add two bay leaves, the zest of one lemon, 12 to 15 peppercorns, 1 teaspoon of blade mace, and a moderate amount of salt to suit your taste.

Add two cups of cold water, put the lid on the pan and let the contents steam slowly for two and a half to three hours, adding more water if it becomes dry. When fully cooked, take the beef, onion, and carrots out and place them on a hot dish to keep it warm.

Skim the liquid in the pan, thicken it with flour, and squeeze the juice from the zested lemon into it. Bring the liquid to a boil and let it begin to thicken, strain some of the liquid over the meat on its platter, and serve the remainder in a sauceboat.

Right: Official state of Texas longhorn herd located at Fort Griffin State Historic Site, Albany, Texas.

FROM OPEN RANGE TO HISTORIC HERDS: THE LONGHORN'S LEGACY

Over five centuries have passed since the Spanish brought cattle to North America. As those early breeds escaped the missions and settlements from the southeast through the west, they adapted to their environments and flourished. One of these new breeds became known as the Texas Longhorn. Its size, lean build, and long curved horns, some extending up to 120 inches from tip to tip, made the Longhorn well-adapted to its life in the southwest.

Early Texas ranches were stocked with wild cattle roaming the open range. Given their hardy dispositions, they were well suited to survive the drives along the Western, Chisolm, and Goodnight-Loving trails to the vast railyards of Kansas, Wyoming, and other northern states. By 1895, the great northern trails fell into disuse, the Longhorns were interbred with other types of cattle, and the Longhorn population declined. Today, the Texas Historical Commission and Texas Parks and Wildlife maintain the state's official herd of genetically pure and historically correct Texas Longhorns. You can visit this legacy breed of cattle at Fort Griffin State Historic Site, Copper Breaks, San Angelo, Palo Duro Canyon, and LBJ state parks.

20TH CENTURY TEXAS

As Texas entered the 20th century, its foodways continued to reflect the state's complex cultural and historical evolution, and its expansion into more mainstream modern cuisine. With the arrival of new populations, particularly from the Gulf States, Mexico, and other regions, Texas food became an even richer and more vibrant reflection of its people. The post-World War II era brought rapid urbanization in cities like Houston, Dallas, and San Antonio, further contributing to the state's culinary development.

The spread of "Tex-Mex" cuisine, which evolved from Spanish, Mexican, and Indigenous food traditions, became a national phenomenon in the 1940s and 1950s. The mass production of food products and advancements in transportation, especially the expansion of the railroad system, played a crucial role in the dissemination of these culinary trends.

The 1960s and '70s also brought many immigrants from the far east, primarily from Vietnam, Cambodia, Thailand, and India. The newcomers adapted to new ingredients found here and influenced the ever-widening availability of global cuisines to Texans, particularly in large cities and urban areas.

By the late 20th century, Texas foodways had become a rich and complex tapestry. Local traditions blended with global trends and new culinary experiments, making Texas one of the most dynamic and innovative food cultures in the United States. The state's food culture remains a testament to its remarkable history and its ability to adapt and grow with the changing times.

SIDE DISHES AND VEGETABLES

AMERICAN POTATO SALAD
STARR FAMILY HOME STATE HISTORIC SITE

Historical Note:

Recipe adapted from ***Practical American Cookery and Household Management****, Julia Corson, 1886.*

INGREDIENTS:

6 cold boiled potatoes, sliced but not too thin
2 hard boiled eggs
1 head of celery
1 onion
1 raw egg yolk
1 gill of oil (4 oz.)
2 T. vinegar
1 level tsp. each of salt and dry mustard
1 saltspoonful pepper (¼ tsp.)

PROCESS:

Peel half a dozen cold boiled potatoes, and slice them, not too thin. Boil two eggs hard. Wash, and chop rather fine one head of celery. Peel one onion, and chop it fine. Break the yolks of the hard-boiled eggs smooth with the yolk of one raw egg; stir with them a gill of oil, two tablespoonfuls of vinegar, a level teaspoonful each of salt and dry mustard, and a saltspoonful of pepper; mix this dressing with the potato, celery, and onion, and serve the salad.

BAKED PEAS
SAM RAYBURN HOUSE STATE HISTORIC SITE

Historical Note:

This recipe, often made by Minnie Eldridge, a second cousin to Sam Rayburn, was published in ***The Fannin County Home Demonstration Club Cookbook*** *published in 1933 and dedicated to Miss Eldridge.*

INGREDIENTS:

6 slices bacon
2 C. canned peas
1 C. rich milk
1 tsp. salt
½ tsp. pepper
½ C. bread crumbs

PROCESS:

Cut bacon in small pieces and cook until crisp. Add the peas, milk, salt, and pepper. Put in a greased casserole dish and cover with bread crumbs. Bake in a moderate oven 20 minutes. Serves six.

GRAPE DUMPLINGS (CONTEMPORARY VERSION)

CADDO MOUNDS STATE HISTORIC SITE

Historical Note:

A traditional dessert, grape dumplings make a deep purple, juicy pastry dish. These dark purple dumplings have a sweet taste that is reminiscent of home for many Native Americans.

INGREDIENTS:

2 C. all-purpose flour
1 egg
1¼ C. water
64 oz. grape juice
Sugar to taste
1 T. cornstarch
1 C. water

PROCESS:

Place flour in a heap on tabletop. Make a well in center of flour and crack an egg into center. Using a fork, begin mixing the egg into the flour and add water as you go. Form the dough into a ball and roll out very thin. Cut into 1-inch squares.

In a large pot place grape juice and sugar to taste. Bring to a rolling boil. Drop dumplings into boiling grape juice. Mix 1 tablespoon cornstarch in 1 cup water. Add to the hot grape juice. Cook for a few minutes and serve hot.

CABBAGE SALAD

STARR FAMILY HOME STATE HISTORIC SITE

Historical Note:

Recipe adapted from ***Miss Parola's New Cook Book,*** *Maria Parola, 1882.*

INGREDIENTS:

1 large head of cabbage
12 eggs, hard-boiled, divided
2 tsp. dry mustard
2 small cupfuls of sugar
1 C. vinegar or more, if you like
2 tsp. salt
1 T. melted butter
Pickled beets for garnish

PROCESS:

Divide the cabbage into four pieces, and wash well in cold water. Take off all the wilted leaves and cut out the tough, hard parts. Cut the cabbage very fine with a sharp knife. Have the eggs boiled hard, and 10 of them chopped fine. Add these and the other ingredients to the cabbage. Pour 1 tablespoon of melted butter over the cabbage. Arrange on a dish and garnish with the two remaining eggs and pickled beets.

CAULIFLOWER GREENS

SLATON HARVEY HOUSE STATE HISTORIC SITE

Historical Note:

*Recipe from the **Super Chef Cook Book of Famous Fred Harvey Recipes**, Santa Fe Railroad Company, 1946.*

INGREDIENTS:

2 T. chopped onion
3 strips bacon, diced
2 tsp. olive oil
½ C. chopped tomatoes
½ C. tomato puree
½ clove garlic, minced
1 (1-¼ lb.) cauliflower
Grated parmesan cheese (optional)

PROCESS:

Sauté onion and bacon in olive oil until tender but not brown. Add chopped tomatoes, tomato puree, and garlic. Simmer until amount is reduced to half, about 20 minutes. Wash cauliflower, including the good leaves and stems; chop fine. Cook 5 minutes in boiling salted water and drain. Add to tomato sauce and serve. Sprinkle grated Parmesan cheese over each serving, if desired.

Yield: 4 to 6 servings

THE TOMATO.

CORN SUPREME

SAM RAYBURN HOUSE STATE HISTORIC SITE

Historical Note:

*Some of Mr. Sam's favorite foods included watermelon, sweet corn, onion sandwiches, and crumblin' - a concoction of cornbread crumbled in milk! This recipe for sweet corn is found in the 1933 **Fannin County Home Demonstration Club Cookbook**, and was a popular way to serve corn at mealtimes.*

INGREDIENTS:

2 C canned or fresh corn
Butter
1 C. ground cheese
Salt and pepper to taste
1 C. milk

PROCESS:

Mix all of the ingredients together and bake in a slow oven (300-325 degrees) for about 45 minutes.

Bountiful harvest at Barrington Living History Farm State Historic Site, Washington, Texas.

HOPPIN JOHN
FORT LANCASTER & BATTLEFIELD STATE HISTORIC SITE

Hoppin John, a traditional stew originating with West African traditions brought to America with enslaved people, is mentioned in Frederick Law Olmsted's 19th century travelog of the American South and Texas where he writes,

"The greatest luxury with which they are acquainted is a stew of bacon and peas, with red pepper, which they call 'Hopping John'."

All of the ingredients for Hoppin John would have been available to soldiers at West Texas forts from the late 1850s on.

INGREDIENTS:

2 C. red field peas
1 small dried hot red chili
Fresh herbs, like sage, rosemary, and thyme
Bacon· chopped into large pieces
2 tsp. kosher salt
Red chili flakes
1 tsp. black pepper
2 onions, plus 1 more
Chicken or ham broth
1¼ C. Carolina rice (or any other white rice)

PROCESS:

Pick through the field peas and discard any shriveled or broken peas and any debris. Put them in a large bowl and fill it with cold water. Stir several times and discard any peas that float to the top. Let the field peas soak for 30 minutes.

Bring 6 cups of salted water to a boil in a large pot. Add the field peas, chili, and herbs (leave them whole) to the water. Cover and boil for 15 minutes, then reduce heat to a low boil for 25 minutes. The peas should be softer, but still firm and not mushy.

After the field peas have cooked, take out the dried chili. Strain the liquid out of the field peas and save it for cooking the rice. Put the field peas into the same pot that you cooked the bacon and onions in. Fish out the stems from the herbs. Add a little black pepper. Stir until the peas are coated in the fat.

Break out a cast iron pot if you have one and fry the bacon until it's brown and crisp. Add a small pinch of salt, a small pinch of red chili flakes, and a small pinch of black pepper. When crisp, take the bacon out and put it on a paper towel lined plate to drain.

Cut the remaining onion in half and add it to the pot, along with the low sodium broth, enough to cover the peas. Add ¼ cup of the crisped bacon and bring the pot to a boil. Reduce to a simmer and cook for 1 hour. Be careful not to let them burn or get too low on liquid. The peas should be tender but not overly mushy or cracked.

Rinse the rice well. Put it in a pot and add the reserved liquid from the field peas. Add enough water so that the water comes up 1" above the level of the rice. Bring to a simmer, then cover and cook for 45 minutes to 1 hour, or until dry. When everything is ready, mix together the warm rice and peas, remaining crisped bacon, and the lightly fried onion. Stir well, and serve it forth for good luck in the New Year.

KARTOFFELN MIT APFELS (POTATOES WITH APPLES)

KREISCHE BREWERY STATE HISTORIC SITE

Historical Note:

Recipe adapted from ***German Cookery,*** *Ella Oswald, 1906.*

INGREDIENTS:

2 lbs. potatoes
Salted water
2 lbs. apples
Salt and sugar to taste
Butter
2 oz. bacon, diced

PROCESS:

Peel the potatoes, cut them into quarters, boil in water with salt, drain and partly mash them.

Meanwhile cut the apples and boil them to a pulp and then mix well with the potatoes, flavoring with salt, sugar, and butter to taste.

Dice the bacon, fry it until the fat is melted, and pour over the dish. In some areas fresh plums, prunes, or pears are prepared with potatoes the same way.

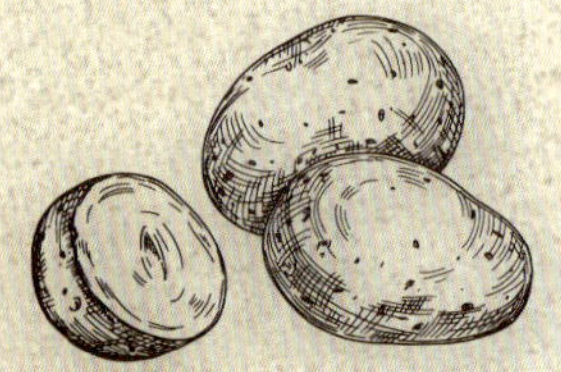

PAN KALE

FRENCH LEGATION STATE HISTORIC SITE

Historical Note:

Recipe adapted from ***Mrs. Beaton's Book of Household Management****, Isabella Beaton, 1861.*

INGREDIENTS:

2 lbs. of Savoy greens
2 qts. water
½ C. oatmeal for thickening
¼ lb. of butter or bacon drippings
Salt and pepper to taste

PROCESS:

Chop the Savoy cabbage very fine. Bring the water to a slow boil and thicken it with the oatmeal. Put the cabbage and butter drippings in the pot and simmer for 1-1/2 hours. Season with salt and pepper.

POTATO PIE

ACTON STATE HISTORIC SITE

Historical Note:

This kind of recipe, using hardy staple produce that could be kept year-round often made up a major part of the diet of many households in the Upper South, including Kentucky where the Crocketts lived. Recipe adapted from ***The Cook's Oracle,*** *William Kitchiner, 1829.*

INGREDIENTS:

1 small onion
4 hard-boiled egg yolks
5 to 7 white waxy potatoes
Salt and pepper to taste
2 to 3 T. water
2 oz. cold butter cut into small pieces
Pie dough to make a top-crust only pie

PROCESS:

Chop the onion very fine. Chop the egg yolks very fine. Wash and peel the potatoes, and cut them very thin. Begin layering the potatoes in your pie pan placing a layer of chopped onion between each layer with a little salt and pepper. Once the pie pan is full add two to three tablespoons of water. Top with the chopped egg yolks and small pieces of butter. Cover the pie pan with the dough and cut small slits to help vent steam. Bake at 325 degrees for an hour to an hour and a half, until the potatoes yield well to a thin knife inserted through the top crust.

POTATOES STEWED WHOLE

FRENCH LEGATION STATE HISTORIC SITE

Historical Note:

Recipe adapted from ***Domestic French Cookery, Chiefly Translated from Sulpice Barué,*** *Miss Eliza Leslie, 1836. This was the first French Cookbook translated for the American Market.*

INGREDIENTS:

2 dozen small new potatoes
1 piece of butter rolled in flour
Half the peel of a lemon, grated
Half a nutmeg, grated
Salt
2-3 lumps* of sugar
3 tsp. sweet oil*
Juice from one lemon

PROCESS:

Boil two dozen small new potatoes with some salt. Put into a stew-pan a piece of butter rolled in flour, half the peel of a lemon grated, half a nutmeg grated, some salt, two to three lumps of sugar, and three tea spoonfuls of sweet oil. Lay the potatoes in this mixture, squeeze over them the juice of a lemon, and let them stew gently about 10 minutes.

*For this recipe, you can consider a saucepan to be a stew-pan. Sweet oil is akin to olive oil or vegetable oil, and a lump of sugar is about the size of a tablespoon.

ROTKOHL (RED CABBAGE)

KREISCHE BREWERY STATE HISTORIC SITE

Historical Note:

Recipe adapted from ***German Cookery,*** *Ella Oswald, 1906.*

INGREDIENTS:

4 lbs. red cabbage
2 T. vinegar
4 oz. of lard (or vegetable fat)
2 apples or pears
2 tsp. chopped onions
2 tsp. ground caraway seed
Salt to taste
½ pt. water
2 oz. of sugar
1 potato, grated

PROCESS:

Chop the cabbage up finely, scald it with boiling water, drain the water off and immediately add 2 tablespoons of vinegar. Melt the lard (or vegetable fat) and stir it into the cabbage. Cut the apples or pears into slices and add them to pot along with the chopped onion, ground caraway seed, and salt. Pour ½ pint of water and simmer for 1-½ to 2 hours. Then add the sugar and a grated raw potato and serve.

The Recipe for Resilience: The Life and Work of Malinda Russell

Malinda Russell's ***A Domestic Cook Book***, published in 1866 and recognized as the first cookbook published by an African American author, is a fascinating first-person chronicle of a free woman of color in mid-19th century America. Hers was a life of hard labor and misfortune, but she overcame her hardships and setbacks with an indomitable spirit. As a free woman who could read and write she recorded her story in her own words, beginning with,

"I was born in Washington County, and raised in Green County, in the eastern part of Tennessee. My mother, Malinda Russell, was a member of one of the first families set free by Mr. Noddie, of Virginia."

Her mother was born after the emancipation of her grandmother, and therefore all her children were free by law. Her mother died when she was quite young. At the age of about 19, Malinda Russell set out for Liberia but was robbed by a member of the party with whom she was traveling. Due to the loss of her travel funds she was forced to stop at Lynchburgh, Virginia, which is where she first began cooking. The following is a certificate given to Malinda by Doctor More at the time she started her trip to Liberia:

"We, the undersigned, have been acquainted with Malinda Russell, a free woman of color, for the last eight or ten years, and certify that she is a girl of fine disposition and business-doing habits. Her moral deportment, of late, has been respectable; and we have little doubt, should she reach Liberia, in Africa; to which place she is now bound, that she will make a valuable citizen."

While in Virginia, Malinda married Anderson Vaughan. They had one child, a boy, who was crippled and only had the use of one hand. Anderson Vaughn passed away four years after they were married, leaving Malinda widowed with a young special needs child to care for. After her husband's death she always used her maiden name. While in Virginia, she also ran a wash house. The following appeared in local papers as an advertisement for her business:

"Malinda Vaughan, Fashionable Laundress, would respectfully inform the ladies and Gentlemen of Abingdon, that she is prepared to wash and iron every description of clothing in the neatest and most satisfactory manner. Every article washed by her, she guarantees shall pass unscathed through the severest ordeal of inspection, without the remotest danger of condemnation. She can conscientiously boast of a proficiency in her business, and all clothing committed to her charge shall be neatly executed and well taken care of. She hopes to receive, as she shall exert herself to deserve, a sufficiency of patronage to insure her a permanent location. Her charges shall correspond with the times. —ABINGDON, May 3."

Sometime after the death of her husband, she moved to Cold Springs, Tennessee near her original home, where she ran a boarding house on Chuckey Mountain for three years. Her boarders came from almost every state in the Union to visit the springs for their health. After leaving the boarding-house, she kept a pastry shop for about six years, and, by hard labor and economy, saved a considerable sum of money for the support of herself and son. During an attack by a Confederate raiding party on January 16, 1864, her life was threatened and her savings were stolen. After being attacked several more times Malinda and her son left and moved to the Northern states.

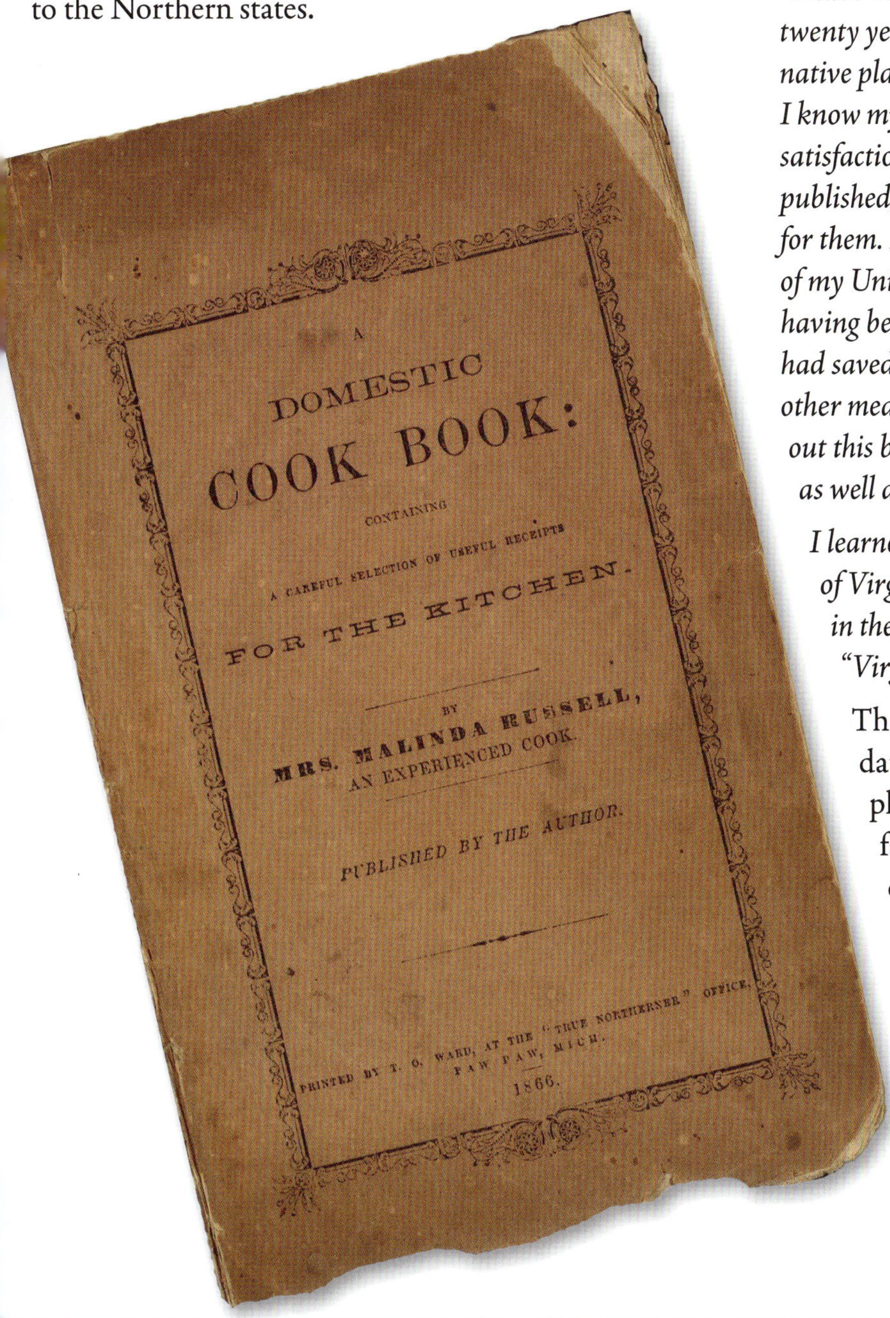
A DOMESTIC

COOK BOOK:

CONTAINING

A CAREFUL SELECTION OF USEFUL RECEIPTS

FOR THE KITCHEN.

BY

MRS. MALINDA RUSSELL,

AN EXPERIENCED COOK.

PUBLISHED BY THE AUTHOR.

PRINTED BY T. O. WARD, AT THE "TRUE NORTHERNER" OFFICE,

PAW PAW, MICH.

1866.

Having heard that Michigan was the Garden of the West, Malinda decided to make it her home until the war was over when she planned to return to Greenville, Tennessee to try and recoup at least a part of her money that had been stolen.

Raising funds is one reason why she published her Cook Book hoping to receive enough from the sale of it to enable her to return home. She felt certain that her book would sell well and that her recipes were nutritious and satisfying. Malinda Russell's Cook Book was published in May, 1866 in Paw-Paw, Michigan. In the introduction she wrote,

"I have made Cooking my employment for the last twenty years, in the first families of Tennessee, (my native place,) Virginia, North Carolina, and Kentucky. I know my Receipts to be good, as they always have given satisfaction. I have been advised to have my Receipts published, as they are valuable, and every family has use for them. Being compelled to leave the South on account of my Union principles, in the time of the Rebellion, and having been robbed of all my hard-earned wages which I had saved; and as I am now advanced in years, with no other means of support than my own labor; I have put out this book with the intention of benefiting the public as well as myself.

I learned my trade of Fanny Steward, a colored cook, of Virginia, and have since learned many new things in the art of Cooking. I cook after the plan of the "Virginia Housewife.""

There has been no record found listing the date of Malinda Russell's death, nor her place of burial. What she left behind is her fascinating and historically important cookbook.

Site interpreter harvesting at Barrington Living History Farm State Historic Site, Washington, Texas.

Right: Chief of Interpretation, Hal Simon, and volunteer interpreter conducting foodways programming at French Legation State Historic Site, Austin, Texas.

Sauces and Gravies

BARBARA BUSH'S BARBECUE SAUCE

BUSH FAMILY HOME STATE HISTORIC SITE

Historical Note:

This is one of the recipes that First Lady Barbara Bush shared widely among her family and friends. It pairs very well with barbecued beef, pork, or chicken.

INGREDIENTS:

¼ C. cider vinegar
2¼ C. water
¾ C. sugar
1 stick butter, unsalted
⅓ C. yellow mustard
2 medium onions, chopped
½ tsp. each, salt and pepper
½ C. Worcestershire sauce
2½ C. ketchup
7 to 8 tsp. lemon juice
Dash cayenne pepper

PROCESS:

In a pot, combine cider vinegar, water, sugar, butter, yellow mustard, onions, salt, and pepper. Bring to a boil, cook over low heat until onions are tender, about 20 minutes. Add the remaining ingredients, stir and simmer slowly for 45 minutes. Freezes and cans well.

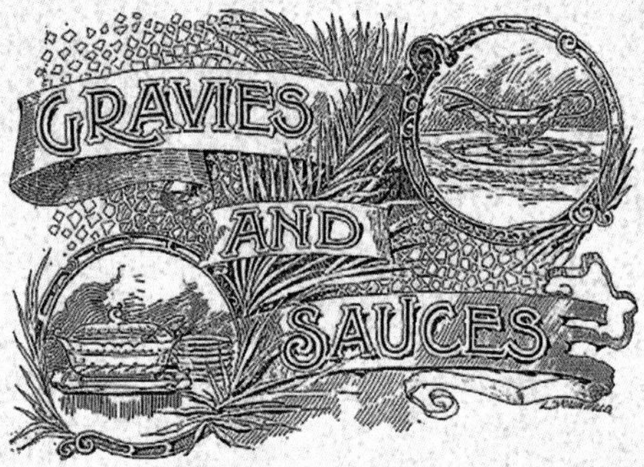

MOLE VERDE

CASA NAVARRO STATE HISTORIC SITE

Historical Note:

*A series of cookbooks was published in Mexico and distributed in San Antonio in the early 20th century. This recipe was featured in **La Cocina en el Bolsillo**. It is likely that the residents of Laredito, the neighborhood where Casa Navarro is located, would have used recipes from this cookbook or similar ones. Green mole is a sauce used in cooking many Mexican dishes.*

INGREDIENTS:

10 tomatillos, husked and halved
5-10 jalapeño or poblano peppers
2 T. cumin seed
1 C. shelled pumpkin seeds
1 T. canola oil
Chicken or turkey broth

PROCESS:

Chop and roast tomatillos and peppers. Remove skins from tomatillos. Grind both with a molcajete. Fry cumin seed and pumpkin seed in canola oil, let cool and grind with a molcajete. Place ground tomatillos, peppers, cumin seed, and pumpkin seed in large pot, add broth and simmer for 15 minutes. Use this sauce for enchiladas, put it inside of tamales, or cook pork in it.

PESTLE AND MORTAR.

PASILLA CHILE WITH VINEGAR SALSA PASILLA

CASA NAVARRO STATE HISTORIC SITE

Historical Note:

*This recipe is from **La Concina en el Bolsillo, Book #8**, a collection of cookbooks published in the late 19th century. These cookbooks were small and could fit in your bolsillo or pocket. Several editions were published between 1890 and 1909.*

INGREDIENTS:

4 pasilla peppers, roasted in oil
5 garlic cloves
Vinegar
Salt to taste
Cinnamon to taste
½ large onion, chopped
Olive oil

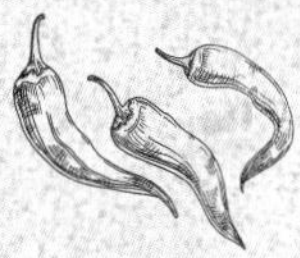

PROCESS:

Roast the pasilla peppers until they break open and remove the seeds. Finely grind pasilla chiles and garlic in a molcajete. This will create a thick paste. Thin with vinegar. Add salt and cinnamon to taste. Add chopped onion and stir in oil. If fresh pasilla peppers cannot be used, dried pasilla can be substituted. Fresh versus dried peppers will determine the amount of liquid necessary to thin the paste base.

RUM CATCHUP

WASHINGTON-ON-THE-BRAZOS STATE HISTORIC SITE

Historical Note:

*This recipe was transcribed from **The Kentucky Housewife**, Lettice Bryan, 1839. "Catchup" originally referred to any sauce created for using on cooked meats. Some of the earliest uses of the word described an East Indian sauce made with fruits and spices might be from the Tulu word "**kajipu,**" meaning "**curry**" and said to derive from "**kaje,**" meaning "**to chew.**" Yet the word, usually spelled ketchup, is also described in early use as something resembling anchovy or soy sauce. In 19th century cookbooks many different catchup recipes include mushroom catchup, green walnut catchup, and oyster catchup. Tomato catchup first appears around 1800 in the United States, and by 1920 the spelling was standardized to "ketchup" and was exclusively made with tomatoes.*

INGREDIENTS:

Thyme
Parsley
Basil
Sweet Marjoram
Zest of two oranges
Zest of one lemon
½ oz. black pepper
¼ oz. of cayenne pepper
¼ ounce of cloves
1 qt. vinegar
1 Tbsp salt
1 C. Madera wine
1 C. rum

PROCESS:

Put all spice ingredients in a pan with the vinegar, cover it and boil it for a few minutes to extract the flavors of the spices. Strain the mixture and add salt, stirring until well dissolved. Set the mixture aside to cool, after which add Madera wine and rum. Put in small bottles and secure the tops as tightly as possible. This catchup can be used to flavor sauces and gravies or sent to the table for use just as prepared.

SHALLOT OR ONION SAUCE (SAUCE RAVIGOTE)

FRENCH LEGATION STATE HISTORIC SITE

Historical Note:

Recipe is adapted from ***Domestic French Cookery, Chiefly Translated from Sulpice Barué****, Miss Eliza Leslie, 1836. This was the first French cookbook translated for the American market.*

INGREDIENTS:

1 handful of sweet herbs
1 handful of shallots or little onions
Vinegar
Salt to taste
Pepper to taste
Broth or warm water
1 small piece of butter, rolled in flour or one spoonful of olive oil

PROCESS:

Take a handful of sweet herbs and the same quantity of shallots or little onions, and cut them up small. Put them into a saucepan, with some vinegar, salt, pepper, and sufficient broth or warm water to cover them. Take the sauce from the fire and set it on the stove, or on the hearth, and stir in (till it melts) a piece of butter rolled in flour, or a spoonful of olive oil.

RECIPE NOTE:

Measuring ingredients for recipes from more than 100 years ago can be challenging. Many times the recipes were simple guidelines and how many or how much of an ingredient was left entirely up to the cook! We hope you give this one a try and record your measurements on this page, or in the notes section found near the index at the back of this book.

BREADS, BISCUITS AND ROLLS

BATTER BREAD
FULTON MANSION STATE HISTORIC SITE

Historical Note:

This recipe is from Elinor Fulton Conger, Harriett Fulton's granddaughter. She was called Lalla.

INGREDIENTS:

⅔ C. corn meal
1 pt. warm milk
Pinch of salt
1 egg
1 sizeable lump of butter

PROCESS:

Stir ⅔ cup of corn meal into one pint of warm milk. Do this before the milk boils, then it won't lump. After it comes to a boil, remove it from the fire. Add a pinch of salt and beat in 1 whole egg. Pour into a buttered casserole dish and bake in a hot oven until puffed and brown, about 20 minutes. A pretty touch is a sizeable lump of butter in the center before baking.

RECIPE NOTE:

A hot oven is 400-450 degrees.

"Old Martin Varner used to tell a good story of his little son's first experience with a biscuit. The old man had managed to get together money or pelts enough to buy a barrel of flour. Mrs. Varner made a batch of biscuits, which were doubtless heavy as lead and hard as wood. Mrs. Varner set them on the table. The boy looked at them curiously, helped himself to one and made for the door with it. In a few minutes, he came back for another. Doubting the child's ability to eat so quickly, the old man followed him to see what disposition he made of the second. The ingenious youngster had conceived a novel and not altogether illogical idea of their utility. He had punched holes through the center, inserted an axle and triumphantly displayed a miniature Mexican cart. And I assure you, from my recollection of those pioneer biscuits, they were capable of sustaining a pretty heavy load..."

Noah Smithwick, in his memoir Evolution of a State

BISCUITS
VARNER-HOGG PLANTATION STATE HISTORIC SITE

Historical Note:

Recipe redacted from ***The Virginia Housewife****, Mary Randolph, 1824. The simplicity and versatility of the biscuit made it a convenient and economical food for families, and the inclusion of the recipe in "The Virginia Housewife" indicates that biscuits were a common part of the Southern breakfast table. Mary Randolph's recipe is one of the earliest written records of the preparation of biscuits in the Southern United States.*

INGREDIENTS:

2 C· all-purpose flour
2 tsp· baking powder
½ tsp· salt
4 T· unsalted butter· chilled
¾ C· buttermilk

PROCESS:

In a large mixing bowl, whisk together the flour, baking powder, and salt. Cut the butter into the flour mixture using a pastry cutter or your fingers until the mixture resembles coarse crumbs. Add the buttermilk and stir until the dough comes together. Turn the dough out onto a lightly floured surface and roll out to about ½ inch thickness. Cut the dough into rounds using a biscuit cutter or the rim of a glass. Place the biscuits onto a baking sheet lined with parchment paper. Bake at 450 degrees for 12-15 minutes, or until the biscuits are lightly golden brown on top. Serve hot with butter, jelly, or gravy.

BREAD MAKING
FORT GRIFFIN
STATE HISTORIC SITE

Historical Note:

Fort Griffin's bakery was one of the most substantial buildings on the post. It is one of the few structures that remains from the original fort. As bread was a permanent feature of the garrison's diet, the bakery produced 800 loaves per day. Enlisted men assigned to work in the bakery worked weekly for extra duty pay of .35 cents per day.

INGREDIENTS:

4 C. lukewarm water
2 T. yeast
4 C. unsifted flour
5 C. lukewarm water
2 T. salt
7-9 C. flour
Flour for dusting
Lard for greasing pans and warm loaves

RECIPE NOTE:

This recipe will make approximately eight 18-ounce loaves. Place bread in storage 24 to 48 hours prior to issuing to troops. By orders of Major J. L. Fields, L. Wesley Cooke, 2nd Leut. 11th Infantry, Post Adjutant.

PROCESS:

Into a bowl pour four cups of lukewarm water. Dissolve two tablespoons of yeast, then mix in four cups of unsifted flour. Let mixture sit covered with a towel in a warm place for one hour. Then add five more cups of lukewarm water, two tablespoons of salt, and seven to nine cups flour until doughy consistency is reached. Mix well kneading in bowl. Set aside in warm place for one hour, covered. Remove and knead dough on a flat, lightly floured surface. Return dough to bowl, coat surface with lard and set aside for one hour. Then knead dough lightly, cut into eight 18-ounce loaves. Place into greased pans, coat loaves again lightly with lard. Cover and let rise. When sufficiently raised, place pans in oven preheated to 400 degrees. Bake 30 to 45 minutes or until golden brown. Remove loaves from the oven, coat freshly baked bread with lard.

EGG CORN BREAD

WASHINGTON-ON-THE-BRAZOS STATE HISTORIC SITE

Historical Note:

*This recipe was adapted from **What Mrs. Fisher Knows About Old Southern Cooking, Soups, Pickles, Preserves, Etc.**, Abby Fisher, 1881. Mrs. Fisher was a formerly enslaved woman who had lived in the Carolinas and Louisiana. In 1877, she moved her family to San Francisco, California where she taught cooking classes and eventually opened Mrs. Abby Fisher & Co. a pickle and preserves manufacturing firm.*

INGREDIENTS:

2 eggs
1 pt. cornmeal
½ pt. sour milk
1 tsp. baking soda
1 T. melted lard or butter

PROCESS:

Beat two eggs lightly and combine with one pint of meal, half pint of sour milk, one teaspoonful of soda, one tablespoon of melted lard or butter, mix all together, well stirred or beaten. Bake in an ordinary pan.

RECIPE NOTE:

No oven temperature or length of baking time was listed for this recipe. We suggest a 350° oven for 30-40 minutes. Bake Kettles (Dutch ovens) will vary depending on the amount of coals used.

HARD TACK

FORT MARTIN SCOTT STATE HISTORIC SITE

Historical Note:

*This recipe derives from the description of hard tack in the memoir a Union soldier published later in his life, **Hardtack and Coffee**, John Billings 1887. As a foodstuff there isn't really a single recipe for hard tack. Whatever wheat flour that was available, salt, and water were combined to make a clay-like dough.*

INGREDIENTS:

4 C. flour
2 tsp. salt (optional)
Less than 2 C. water

PROCESS:

Mix the flour and salt together in bowl. Add just enough water (less than 2 cups) so that the dough will stick together in a stiff, clay-like texture. Knead the dough by hand. Roll the dough into rectangles using a rolling pin, then cut into squares about 3x3" and about ½" thick. Press a pattern of four rows of four holes into each square using a nail, toothpick or pointed chopstick. Make sure not to punch through the dough. Place hardtack on ungreased cookie sheet and bake at 400 degrees for 20-25 minutes per side. The final hardtack should be slightly brown on each side. Cool on a wire rack or butcher's paper. The fresh crackers are easily broken, but will harden as they continue to dry out. If kept clean and dry, hardtack will last for years.

MRS. E'S SODA BISCUITS
FORT MCKAVETT STATE HISTORIC SITE

Historical Note:

This recipe is from the handwritten cookbook of Alice Kirk Grierson. Her husband commanded Fort Concho, and likely visited Fort McKavett in the 1870s.

INGREDIENTS (15 BISCUITS):

1 tsp. baking soda
2 tsp. cream of tartar
1 tsp. salt
1 qt. flour
2 heaping T. lard
2 C. sweet milk, or you can take can milk

PROCESS:

Rub baking soda, cream of tartar, and salt into flour dry. Next the lard. Lastly the milk. Work with as little handling as possible. The dough should be very soft. Cut more than half inch thick and bake in a quick oven. A quick oven is between 375-400 degrees.

INGREDIENTS (30 BISCUITS):

2 C. flour
1 tsp. cream of tartar
½ tsp. baking soda
½ tsp salt
2 T. lard or margarine
¾ to 1 C. milk

PROCESS:

Sift dry ingredients together. Add lard or margarine and cut into flour mixture. Add milk, a little at a time, stirring with a fork. Add as much of the milk as necessary to make a very soft dough. Roll out ½ inch thick and cut with a small biscuit cutter. Bake at 425 degrees for 15-20 minutes.

OLD VIRGINIA BEATEN BISCUITS

VARNER-HOGG PLANTATION STATE HISTORIC SITE

Historical Note:

This recipe was adapted from ***Domestic Cookery, Useful Receipts, and Hints to Young Housekeepers****, Elizabeth Ellicott Lea, 1845.*

INGREDIENTS:

- 1 qt. flour
- 1 heaping tsp. salt
- 2 T. of butter and lard, evenly mixed
- 1 pt. of milk

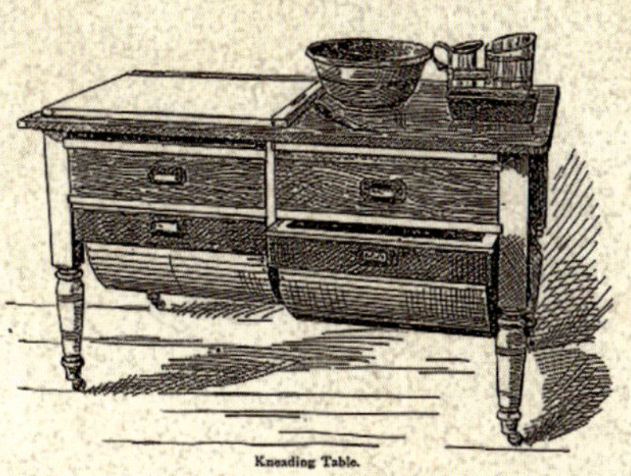

PROCESS:

Combine the ingredients using only enough milk to make a stiff dough. Work the dough a little by hand, and then lay it on a floured surface and beat it with a wooden mallet, meat tenderizer, or flatiron until it forms blisters. Roll the dough out to the size you wish and cut rounds with a biscuit cutter or drinking glass. Prick the top of each with a fork. Bake in a 350 degree oven until golden brown on top. Serve warm.

PLANTATION CORN BREAD OR HOE CAKE

BARRINGTON LIVING HISTORY FARM STATE HISTORIC SITE

Historical Note:

As with most of the recipes from the era, specific baking times and temperatures fluctuated depending on the types of implements being used and the baker's preferences. The name Hoe Cake refers to the type of flat pan that was used to bake the cakes. Charity, who was an enslaved cook at the Barrington Farm, would have made these types of cakes.

INGREDIENTS:

½ T. lard
1 tsp. soda
1 pt. meal (cornmeal)
1 teacup of boiling water (6 oz.)

PROCESS:

Mix half tablespoon of lard and baking soda into a pint of meal, add one teacup of boiling water. Stir well and bake on a hot griddle.

SWEET POTATO CORN BREAD

LEVI JORDAN PLANTATION STATE HISTORIC SITE

Historical Note:

Recipe adapted from ***The Carolina Housewife****, Sarah Rutledge, 1847.*

INGREDIENTS:

2 large sweet potatoes
½ lb. butter
2½ cups brown sugar
8 eggs
1 C. milk
1 qt. fine corn meal

PROCESS:

Peel, boil, and mash the sweet potatoes. Mix the butter, sugar, and cream until smooth. Beat the eggs and stir them into the mixture. Add the milk and stir, then add the corn meal. Beat it all together until it makes a thick batter. Pour into a greased 9" cake pan and bake at 400 degrees for 35-40 minutes, until a knife blade comes out clean. Cool 10-15 minutes before cutting.

VIRGINIA SPOON BREAD

FULTON MANSION STATE HISTORIC SITE

Historical Note:

This is an old recipe and was contributed by Harriett Fulton's great- granddaughter.

INGREDIENTS:

2 C. water
1 C. cornmeal
¼ C. bacon fat (butter or margarine can be substituted for bacon fat)
¾ tsp. salt
3 eggs
1 tsp. baking powder
1 C. milk

PROCESS:

Mix water and cornmeal in a saucepan. Bring slowly to boiling point. Cook 5 minutes or until thick. Add bacon fat, salt, well-beaten eggs, baking powder, and milk. Bake in well-greased square baking dish at 400 degrees for 40 minutes. Serves 6.

Making Unfermented Bread.

WHOLE WHEAT CRACKERS
SAM RAYBURN HOUSE STATE HISTORIC SITE

Historical Note:

This recipe was often made by Minnie Eldridge, a second cousin to Sam Rayburn. It was published in a cookbook dedicated to her entitled, ***Fannin County Home Demonstration Club Cookbook*** *in 1933.*

INGREDIENTS:

2 C. whole wheat flour
3 T. sugar
1 tsp. salt
½ tsp soda
3 T. fat
2 tsp. molasses
6 T. water

PROCESS:

Mix dry ingredients; put in fat, mix molasses and water with dry ingredients. Roll, spread in pan, cut in squares and cook slowly until crisp.

Volunteer interpreters conducting foodways programming during the San Jacinto Fall Fandango event where families and friends are invited to join site staff and explore life on the Texas frontier. San Jacinto Battleground State Historic Site, La Porte, Texas.

Educator and Interpreter, Chandler Wahrmund, brewing coffee at San Felipe de Austin State Historic Site, San Felipe, Texas.

Desserts and Sweets

BREAD FRITTERS
FRENCH LEGATION STATE HISTORIC SITE

Historical Note:

Recipe adapted from ***Domestic French Cookery****, Chiefly Translated from Sulpice Barué, Miss Eliza Leslie, 1836. This was the first French cookbook translated for the American Market.*

INGREDIENTS:

1 qt. of milk
Cinnamon and sugar to taste
1 T. rosewater
Bread slices
Egg yolks, well beaten
Butter, for frying
Powdered sugar

PROCESS:

Boil a quart of milk with cinnamon and sugar to your taste. When done, stir in a tablespoon of rosewater. Cut some slices of bread into a circular shape. Soak them in the milk till they have absorbed it. Then drain them. Have ready some yolks of eggs well beaten. Dip the slices of bread into it, and fry them in butter. Serve them up strewed with powdered sugar.

RECIPE NOTE:

Rosewater was used as a flavoring. It was made by steeping rose petals in water. The rosewater can be substituted with orange blossom water, vanilla, lavender, cinnamon, cardamom, or pandan.

Lead Educator and Interpreter, Nicole Shadle, preparing biscuits at San Felipe de Austin State Historic Site, San Felipe, Texas.

CACTUS FRUIT JELLY
NATIONAL MUSEUM OF THE PACIFIC WAR STATE HISTORIC SITE

Historical Note:

Admiral Nimitz's mother's recipe for Cactus Fruit Jelly from early days in Texas. The Hawaiians called it Panini jelly.

INGREDIENTS:

Cactus fruit
½ C. water
4 C. cactus fruit juice
3½ C. sugar
Juice of two lemons
½ bottle of Certo

RECIPE NOTE:

Certo is used for thickening jellies and jams. It mainly contains fruit pectin from citrus peels like lemons and oranges. Pectin when mixed with acid and sugar is known to form into a gel-like consistency. Certo can be located in the baking aisles of most grocery stores.

PROCESS:

Pick half-ripe cactus fruit with long-handled meat fork to avoid spines. Place in a pail and let water run into it to clean the fruit. Put the fruit in a big pot, spines and all, and slice it to clean the fruit. Add half a cup of water and cook until the fruit is well done. Then, put it in a strainer and strain out the juice, straining several times through a double flour sack.

Boil juice, sugar, and lemon juice for half an hour, then put Certo in and boil again for five minutes. Pour into sterilized glass jars and let set overnight. If the substance does not jell, boil again for 10 minutes.

CHERRY PIE
VARNER-HOGG PLANTATION STATE HISTORIC SITE

Historical Note:

Recipe adapted from ***The Enterprising Housekeeper****, Ellen Louise Johnson, 1898. Cherry was Governor James Hogg's favorite flavor of pie.*

INGREDIENTS:

1 qt. ripe cherries
1½ C. of sugar
1 T. flour
2 pastry crusts

PROCESS:

Stone the cherries, saving the juice. Add the sugar and the flour and stir until well mixed. Line a pie plate with one pastry crust, fill with cherry mix, and cover with the upper crust. When canned cherries are used, take only half the juice to the same amount of cherries, sugar, and flour. Bake for 45-50 minutes in a 350 degree oven.

CLARA WILLOUGHBY'S CARAMEL PIE
STARR FAMILY HOME STATE HISTORIC SITE

Historical Note:

Clara Willoughby was the daughter of Frank and Clara Starr. Mrs. Willoughby inherited Maplecroft, and later granted the property and furnishings to the State of Texas.

INGREDIENTS:

1 lump of butter (1½ to 2 T.)
3 eggs
Butter
1 C. sugar
1 tsp. vanilla
1 T. corn starch
1 C. nuts
1 cooked pastry shell

PROCESS:

In a saucepan, mix butter, sugar, vanilla, corn starch and cook until thick, then add nuts. Put cooked ingredients into cooked pastry. The recipe does not state how long to let the pie set before serving or how to store the pie. We recommend letting the pie set until completely cool and storing any remaining pie lightly covered in the refrigerator.

COLD DESSERT CREAM
LANDMARK INN STATE HISTORIC SITE

Historical Note:

Recipe adapted from ***Mrs. Chadwick's Home Cookery****, Mrs. J. Chadwick, 1853.*

INGREDIENTS:

½ lb. butter
½ lb. sugar
1 to 2 jiggers of bourbon or rum
Grated nutmeg to taste

PROCESS:

Cream together half a pound of butter and half a pound of sugar; Add wine or other spirits and nutmeg to taste. Beat it until it is light and fluffy.

DEWBERRY COBBLER
FANNIN BATTLEGROUND STATE HISTORIC SITE

Historical Note:

Dewberries grow wild in most of Texas and would have been foraged by early settlers as a native fruit source. Patches of wild dewberries grow around Fannin Battleground and are ready to harvest between April and September.

BERRY FILLING INGREDIENTS:

4 C. dewberries, divided
½-¾ C. sugar
½ tsp. lemon zest
Pinch of salt
Grating of nutmeg to taste

TOPPING INGREDIENTS:

1 stick butter or margarine, melted
¾ C. flour
¾ C. sugar
¾ C. milk
2 tsp. baking powder

PROCESS:

Preheat oven to 350 degrees.

Make filling: Put 2 cups of berries, ½ cup sugar, lemon zest, pinch of salt and nutmeg in a medium saucepan. Cook on low, stirring occasionally for about 5 minutes. Using a fork or masher, mash the berries in the pot. (Don't puree the berries; you really want a chunky syrup.) Cook over low/medium heat for a couple of minutes, stirring occasionally. Taste the berry syrup to make sure it is sweet enough for your taste; add more sugar if needed. If the mixture is too thick, you can add a little water to loosen it up. Remove from heat.

In a 9" x 13" casserole dish, pour in the melted butter; then add the flour, sugar, milk, and baking powder. Mix until thoroughly combined. Set it aside. In the saucepan with the syrup, gently stir in the remaining berries (these need to be as intact as possible). Pour berry mixture evenly over the topping. Do not stir. Bake for 45 minutes.

EINSTEIN CAKE
FULTON MANSION STATE HISTORIC SITE

Historical Note:

Recipe from Lalla Rieber, Harriett and George Fulton's granddaughter. Lalla's mother-in-law, Winifred, was a well-known portrait painter. The cake was a collaborative effort of both women and was served to Albert Einstein as he sat for his portrait. He admired it and thereafter was sent one on his birthday for many years.

INGREDIENTS:

1 C. butter
1½ C. sugar
3 eggs
Milk
1 C. flour
½ tsp. cloves
½ tsp. nutmeg
3 tsp. baking powder
1 tsp. cinnamon
½ tsp. allspice
1 C. raisins
½ C. currants
½ C. citron
1 C. nuts (walnuts)
1 C. candied ginger

PROCESS:

Cream the butter and sugar, add eggs and milk, sift together the dry ingredients; fold into butter mixture, then fold in fruits, nuts, and ginger last. Bake for 2 hours at 250 degrees in a fruitcake pan.

Dessert table at Fulton Mansion State Historic Site, Fulton-Rockport, Texas.

ELLA HUBBARD'S PECAN CAKE

CHARLES AND MARY ANN GOODNIGHT RANCH STATE HISTORIC SITE

Historical Note:

Ella Hubbard was the housekeeper for the Goodnights. Her son Cleo was raised on the ranch and grew up to be a cowboy and a rancher. Cleo and his family have continued the legacy that embodies a sense of community that the Goodnights had always fostered. Mr. Goodnight traditionally requested this cake be made every Christmas.

CAKE INGREDIENTS:

2 C. flour
2 tsp. baking powder
¼ tsp. salt
1 C. butter
2 C. sugar
1 C .milk
1 tsp. vanilla
8 egg whites

PROCESS:

Sift flour, measure, and sift three more times with baking powder and salt. Cream the butter, add the sugar; blend well. Blend in the flour mixture, alternate with milk, a little at a time, ending with flour. Add vanilla. Beat egg whites until stiff. Then fold into creamed mixture. Bake in four layers at 350 degrees for 30-35 minutes.

FILLING INGREDIENTS:

2 tsp. cornstarch
1¼ C. sugar
8 egg yolks
1 pt. of hot milk (sweet, or whole milk)
2 C. ground pecans
Pecan halves for decoration

PROCESS:

Mix thoroughly 2 teaspoonfuls of cornstarch with 1¼ cups of sugar. Beat 8 egg yolks and blend with the sugar mixture. Stir this, gradually, into 1 pint of hot milk. Sweet milk in this recipe refers to whole milk. Cook until thick just to spreading consistency. Just before taking off the fire, add 2 cups of ground pecans. Spread between layers and on top and sides. Decorate with pecan halves.

CAKE ICING INGREDIENTS:

2 C. powdered sugar
2 T. prune juice
½ tsp. cinnamon
½ T. lemon juice
⅛ tsp. salt

PROCESS:

Mix all together and spread over the cake.

FRUIT CAKE
SAN JACINTO BATTLEGROUND STATE HISTORIC SITE

Historical Note:

This recipe comes from: Diary, 1858-1859, Allen-Edbon Papers, MC075, San Jacinto Museum and Battlefield Association. Diary of an unknown woman. Based on notes in the diary, she may have been the grandmother of Mrs. Claire (Allen) Edon who was the last surviving member of Houston's founding family.

INGREDIENTS:

1 C. stoned raisins
1 C. currants
1 C. sugar
1 C. flour
1 wine glass of brandy
1 C. citron
Variety of spices

PROCESS:

Rub the stoned raisins in flour before putting into cake, to prevent their sinking to the bottom. Mix all of the ingredients together and bake in a moderate oven. A moderate oven today is 350-375 degrees. How long you bake it for will depend on the size of the baking pan being used. Check the cake after 40 minutes and every 10 minutes after that until done.

RECIPE NOTE:

Stoned raisins are those that have their seeds removed. To stone raisins: Pour boiling water over them and let them stand for five or ten minutes. Drain and rub each raisin between the thumb and finger till the seeds come out clean. Dry the raisins before using them.

FORT LANCASTER FRUITCAKE

FORT LANCASTER & BATTLEFIELD STATE HISTORIC SITE

"The dinner consisted of ham and eggs, elegant rolls and butter, and claret, and I can say that I never tasted better in my life. The dessert took down anything of the kind that I have ever tasted. Peaches preserved, with cream, and fruitcake."

Francell, Lawrence John. Fort Lancaster: ***Texas Frontier Sentinel.***

Historical Note:

Mrs. Laura Carpenter, the wife of Capt. Stephen Decatur Carpenter's (Fort Lancaster Battleground's founder) prepared a fruitcake for the members of Lt. Beale's Camel Expedition in July of 1857. Mays Humphrey Stacey, a 17-year-old traveling with the expedition, recorded the details of Laura Carpenter's dinner and desert:

FRUIT INGREDIENTS:

2 C .raisins
1 C. dates, chopped
2 C. dried apricots, diced
¾ C. rum, brandy, or fruit juice

BATTER INGREDIENTS:

16 T. unsalted butter, at room temperature
2 C. dark brown sugar, packed
¼ C. (85 g.) boiled cider, or dark corn syrup
4 large eggs, at room temperature
3 C. all-purpose flour
1 tsp. baking powder
1 tsp. table salt
1 tsp. cinnamon
¼ tsp. allspice
¼ tsp. nutmeg
½ C. (113 g.) apple juice, orange juice, or water
2 C. chopped, toasted pecans

GLAZE (OPTIONAL):

Brush the warm cake with rum, brandy, simple syrup, or flavored simple syrup (vanilla, rum-flavored, etc.). If you like just a hint of rum or brandy flavor, add 1 tablespoon of liquor to ¾ cup vanilla syrup or simple syrup and brush this mixture on the cakes. (This keeps them moist for weeks; you can skip this step, but they won't stay moist long-term.) When the cakes are completely cool, wrap them tightly in plastic wrap, and store at room temperature for up to 4 to 6 weeks.

PREPARE:

Combine the fruit with the liquid of your choice in a non-reactive bowl; cover and let rest overnight.

PROCESS:

Preheat oven to 350 degrees. Place the butter, sugar, and syrup in a large bowl, and beat together until well combined. Beat in the eggs one at a time, scraping the bowl after each addition. In a separate bowl whisk together the flour, baking powder, salt, and spices. Add the flour mixture to the liquids in the bowl, beating gently to combine. Stir in the juice or water, then the prepared fruit (including any additional liquid that has collected in the bowl), and the nuts. Scrape the bottom and the sides of the bowl, and stir until everything is well combined.

Spoon the batter into the pans, filling them about ¾ full. Bake the cakes on the middle shelf of the oven, as follows: 75 minutes for the medium loaves, and 2 hours + 10 to 15 minutes for the 9" x 5" loaves. The cakes are done when a cake tester inserted into the center comes out clean. Remove the cakes from the oven. Fruitcake can remain in its pan for storage, if desired. Or carefully remove cake from the pan after about 5 minutes, loosening edges first.

GINGER SNAPS

EISENHOWER BIRTHPLACE STATE HISTORIC SITE

Historical Note:

This recipe was adapted from ***Lessons in Cookery, First Mission School of Cookery & Housework****, Mrs. Anna Lowell Woodbury, 1889.*

INGREDIENTS:

½ C. butter
½ C. brown sugar (light)
1 C. molasses
1 tsp. ginger
½ tsp. cinnamon
½ tsp. baking soda
1 scant quart unsifted flour

PROCESS:

Cream the butter with a wooden spoon until light. Cream the sugar into the butter. Add the molasses, ginger, and cinnamon and mix. Dissolve the ½ teaspoon baking soda in one teaspoon of boiling water and add to the butter mix. Sift and mix flour into the mix a little at a time until it becomes stiff, then add the rest of the flour in by hand. Turn onto a well-floured cutting board and roll very thin. Cut into round cakes with a cookie cutter or juice glass. Place on lightly greased cookie sheets and bake at 325 degrees until dark brown.

Kitchen at Eisenhower Birthplace State Historic Site, Dension, Texas.

HARVEY GIRL SPECIAL LITTLE THIN ORANGE PANCAKES

SLATON HARVEY HOUSE STATE HISTORIC SITE

Historical Note:

This recipe is from the ***Super Chef Cook Book of Famous Fred Harvey Recipes****, Santa Fe Railroad Company, 1946. Henry Stovall, author of these tender little cakes, was head vegetable cook in the St. Louis Station. He learned this from his grandmother and passed on to Fred Harvey. Since then, they have been called Harvey Girl Little Thin Orange Pancakes, and they are quite a hit with customers.*

INGREDIENTS:

¼ C. diced orange sections and juice (½ orange)
1 tsp. grated orange peel
1 C. pancake mix
1 C. orange juice (about)

PROCESS:

Combine all ingredients. Bake small pancakes on hot griddle, using 1 tablespoon batter for each pancake. Serve with maple syrup, honey, or jelly. Yield: 12 servings, 3 pancakes per serving.

HOKEY POKEY ICE CREAM

CONFEDERATE REUNION GROUNDS STATE HISTORIC SITE

Historical Note:

Frozen hokey pokey was sold for a penny from pushcarts with an ice cave (freezer compartment), and the customers either licked it from a shallow glass known as a "penny lick" or it was received in a small folded-paper box or hand-wrapped in a piece of waxed paper. The Hokey-Pokey Man, with his barrel pushcart was a regular feature at reunions held at this site. This is not a proper ice cream, but a type of frozen custard made of milk, eggs, sugar, gelatine, and flavoring.

This recipe was adapted from ***The Bread and Biscuit Baker's and Sugar-Boiler's Assistant****, Robert Wells,1890*

INGREDIENTS:

2 oz. of gelatine
8 oz. of water
4 qts. of milk
8 eggs
1½ lbs. of sugar
Rind of 2 lemons
Pinch of salt

PROCESS:

Dissolve the gelatine in 8 ounces of water. Put the ingredients except the dissolved gelatine into a pan and place on a medium heat burner. Stir constantly till it begins to thicken; remove it quickly, and pour it into a ceramic or glass mixing bowl. Continue to stir it till nearly cold, then add and stir in the dissolved gelatine. Pour it into your ice cream freezer and freeze as for other ices.

Interpreters, Laura Fisher and Theresa Herrera, preparing pies at Barrington Living History Farm State Historic Site, Washington, Texas.

INDIAN HASTY PUDDING

WASHINGTON-ON-THE-BRAZOS STATE HISTORIC SITE

Historical Note:

"Indian meal" was a common name used for cornmeal during the 1820s-1840s. This recipe was adapted from ***The Indian Meal Book****, Eliza Leslie, 1846.*

INGREDIENTS:

3 qts. of water
A small tsp. of salt
3 qts (or more) of sifted Indian meal
¼ lb. of fresh butter, cut small

PROCESS:

Put 3 quarts of water into a saucepan, and add a teaspoonful of salt. Bring the water to a full rolling boil. Begin to stir in the Indian meal a cup at a time, until it is very thick and smooth, like a very soft dough, adding the butter pieces as you stir. Continue to boil and stir it, till the spoon will stand upright in the middle. Send it to table hot, and eat it with milk or cream, and either treacle or sugar.

LALA'S ROCK COOKIES
SAM BELL MAXEY HOUSE STATE HISTORIC SITE

Historical Note:

This is a personal recipe of Lala Long. Sam Bell Maxey was a Mexican War veteran, former Confederate general, and future U.S. Senator when his family moved into their fashionable, newly built home on the south side of Paris in 1868. Sam Bell Maxey Long (Maxey's great-nephew) and his wife 'Lala' inherited the home in 1908.

INGREDIENTS:

1 C. sugar
⅔ C. butter, softened
2 eggs beaten
1 tsp. vanilla extract
2½ C. flour
½ tsp. cinnamon
½ tsp. nutmeg
½ tsp. ground cloves
½ tsp. baking soda, dissolved in 1 T. hot water
1 lb. raisins
1 lb. pecans, chopped
Powdered sugar for rolling

PROCESS:

Cream together sugar and butter; add eggs. Mix in vanilla extract. Add flour, seasonings, and baking soda. Mix well; add raisins and pecans. Drop by teaspoonfuls onto greased cookie sheet. Bake at 375 degrees for 15 minutes. When cool, roll in powdered sugar. Allow to harden for at least 3 days before serving.

LAST CHANCE CHOCOLATE PIE
FULTON MANSION
STATE HISTORIC SITE

Historical Note:

Wilfreda Fulton Hoopes Foss made this recipe on special occasions.

INGREDIENTS:

¼ lb. butter
¾ C. granulated sugar
2 eggs
1 oz. melted baking chocolate
1 tsp. vanilla or 2 T. Kahlua
Rich crust or crumb crust made with chocolate wafers
Whipped cream brandy, etc
Shaved chocolate

PROCESS:

All ingredients must be at room temperature. Use a stationary mixer. Cream butter very thoroughly and add the sugar, one tablespoon at a time. Beat 3 to 4 minutes when all has been added. Add eggs separately, beating 3 minutes after each addition. Continue beating the mixture until the sugar has dissolved and mixture does not feel grainy. Stir in the chocolate and flavorings; pour into the prepared shell. Chill for at least 3 hours. Top with flavored whipped cream and shaved chocolate.

LEBKUCHEN GERMAN GINGERBREAD

KREISCHE BREWERY STATE HISTORIC SITE

Historical Note:

This recipe is from a handwritten family cookbook by Franzika Lippart Spiess (1861-1936), and has been handed down through her Spiess and Simon descendants.

INGREDIENTS:

⅔ C. honey
1 C. sugar
⅓ C. butter
1 egg
⅓ C. water
4 C. sifted cake flour
1 tsp. baking soda
½ tsp. salt
1 tsp. cinnamon
1 tsp. cloves
2/3 C. chopped nuts
1/3 C. chopped citron
Confectioners sugar
Lemon juice

PROCESS:

Boil honey, sugar and butter together for 5 minutes; let cool. Beat egg and add to water. Mix and sift flour, soda, salt and spices, and add alternately with liquid ingredients to honey mixture. Add nuts and citron last. Chill. Allow the dough to ripen for five to seven days in a cool dry place or the ice box before rolling out. Roll about 1/4" thick, cut in diamond shape. Bake at 350 degrees for 15-20 minutes. Ice with a sugar glaze made by diluting confectioner's sugar with lemon juice to make it the consistency of thin cream.

LEMON CUPS-LIKE CAKE & CUSTARD

NATIONAL MUSEUM OF THE PACIFIC WAR STATE HISTORIC SITE

Historical Note:

This recipe is from ***Recipes For Today****, published by General Foods Corporation, 1943.*

INGREDIENTS:

1 C. sugar
5 T. flour
1/8 tsp. salt
Juice of 1 lemon
2 egg yolks, beaten
½ C. Carnation Milk mixed with ½ C. water
2 egg whites, beaten stiff

PROCESS:

Mix the sugar, flour and salt. Add the lemon juice, beaten egg yolks, milk and, water. Fold in the beaten egg whites. Turn mixture into greased custard cups. Set in pan of boiling water. Bake in 375 degree oven for 40 minutes. Unmold. Serve hot or cold. Serves 6.

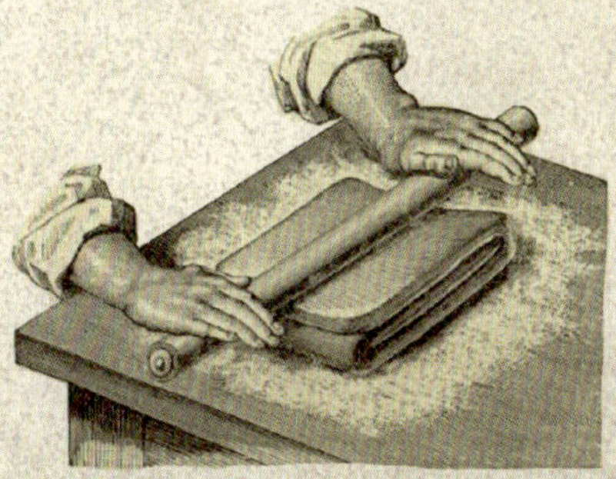

LEMON ORANGE CAKE
NATIONAL MUSEUM OF THE PACIFIC WAR STATE HISTORIC SITE

Historical Note:

Recipe related to the papers of John W. Jones, who served in the 378th Infantry Regiment, 97th Infantry Division during World War II. Jones trained in the US at Camp Wolters and Fort Ord, then was shipped to PTO and Luzon.

INGREDIENTS:

1½ C. sifted cake flour
1 C. sugar
1¾ tsp. baking powder
¼ tsp. salt
½ C. shortening
½ C. milk
2 eggs, beaten
1 tsp. grated orange rind
½ tsp. grated lemon rind

PROCESS:

Store shortening at room temperature. Grease pan, line bottom with waxed paper, and grease again. Use 9"x5"x3" inch loaf pan. Start oven for moderate heat (375 degrees). Sift flour over once before measuring. Stir shortening to soften; Sift in dry ingredients. Add ½ cup of milk and the eggs. Mix until all flour is dampened, then beat for 3 minutes. Pour batter into pan. Bake 30 to 35 minutes for square cake, 50 for loaf, and 20 for cupcakes.

MANDELKUCHEN (ALMOND CAKE)
KREISCHE BREWERY STATE HISTORIC SITE

Historical Note:

This recipe was adapted from ***German Cookery****, Ella Oswald, 1906.*

INGREDIENTS:

¾ lb. butter divided
6 oz. sugar
6 eggs, separated
Grated rind of one lemon
1 lb. flour
½ oz. of baking powder
3 oz. almonds, chopped

PROCESS:

Cream together half of the butter and the sugar. Add the beaten egg yolks and grated lemon peel. In a separate bowl, sift together the flour and baking powder. Add to creamed butter mixture. Whisk the egg whites until they are fluffy and beginning to form peaks; fold into batter. Spread the batter at least a quarter inch thick. Scatter the top with chopped almonds and scatter the remaining butter. Bake in a moderate oven (350 degrees) for about 30 minutes. Cool before cutting.

MOCK APPLE PIE
EISENHOWER BIRTHPLACE STATE HISTORIC SITE

Historical Note:

*This recipe was adapted from **Lessons in Cookery, First Mission School of Cookery & Housework**, Mrs. Anna Lowell Woodbury, 1889.*

INGREDIENTS:

2 C. broken soda cracker pieces
1 C. cold water
1 lemon, grated zest and juice
1 C. sugar
Pie dough to make a double-crust pie

PROCESS:

Soak the cracker pieces in one cup of cold water until it is absorbed. Add the lemon and sugar, stirring them in until smooth and well mixed. Place it all in a pie pan lined with pie dough and cover with top crust. Trim the edges of the dough and crimp closed. Bake in a 375 degree oven until the top crust is golden brown.

MOLASSES PIE

CONFEDERATE REUNION GROUNDS STATE HISTORIC SITE

Historical Note:

This recipe was adapted from ***The Knights of Pythias Oakleaf Temple No. 41 Cookbook,*** *Lyra, TX, 1907. Molasses Pie recipe courtesy of Mrs. Gus Sparling. Pie Crust recipe courtesy of Mrs. G. W. Strawn.*

FILLING INGREDIENTS:

1 C. unsulphered molasses
½ C. sugar
2 eggs
2 T. butter
¼ tsp. nutmeg

CRUST INGREDIENTS:

½ C. butter
½ C. lard or shortening
3 C. flour
¼ tsp. salt
Ice water

PROCESS:

For the crust, combine the butter and lard until well mixed. Add the salt and begin to mix the flour a little at a time, cutting it in with a pastry cutter or two forks. Add ice water in very small amounts until the ingredients all hold together and a desirable pie dough consistency is made. Handle the dough as little as possible. Roll on a lightly floured cutting board on one side only. Line the pie pan and trim dough to the edges. For the filling, mix the molasses, sugar, eggs, butter, nutmeg, and pour into a pie pan lined with the crust. Bake in a 325 degree oven until well set. Cool before serving.

NEW ORLEANS PUDDING

MAGOFFIN HOME STATE HISTORIC SITE

Historical Note:

This recipe was written by Josephine Magoffin Richardson in her private journal dated Tuesday February 18, 1851 as she was preparing for her marriage to Charles Richardson. Her journal contains many tips and tricks for maintaining a household as a pioneer of the West.

INGREDIENTS:

A pre-made sponge cake
Lemon juice or wine
6 eggs, lightly beaten
1 pt. milk or cream
4 T. powdered sugar
½ of a whole nutmeg
Egg whites
Sugar
Lemon juice

PROCESS:

Moisten some sponge cake with lemon juice or wine. Beat 6 eggs, very light, and stir them into a pint of milk or cream; add 4 tablespoonfuls of powdered sugar and half of a whole nutmeg. Mix the whole and bake it brown. When cold, garnish it with beaten whites of eggs thickened with white sugar, and a little lemon juice, then brown the top slightly.

Right: Lead Educator and Interpreter, Jennifer Townzen, conducting foodways programming at Kriesche Brewery State Historic Site, La Grange, Texas.

OLD COLONY BREAD PUDDING

LANDMARK INN STATE HISTORIC SITE

Historical Note:

This recipe was adapted from ***Mrs. Chadwick's Home Cookery****, Mrs. J. Chadwick, 1853.*

INGREDIENTS:

½ lb. chopped and shredded suet or frozen and grated vegetable shortening
1 loaf of stale or lightly toasted bread
1 lb. of chopped apples
1 lb. raisins
½ lb. currants
Nutmeg
Lemon peel
2 quarts milk
12 eggs
Sugar to taste

RECIPE NOTE:

Suet is the raw, hard fat of beef, lamb, or mutton found around the loins and kidneys. Used traditionally in British puddings or savory pies.

PROCESS:

Place a thin layer of suet in a deep baking dish, then a layer of bread, then a layer of fruit. Keep alternating layers of suet, bread, fruit, adding grated nutmeg and lemon peel at each layer until your baking dish is full. Mix a nice custard of milk, eggs, and sugar. Pour it over the layered ingredients, and place it in the refrigerator for one and a half to two hours. Let it come back to almost room temperature and bake in a 350 degree oven for about two hours, or until a straw pulls out clean.

ORANGE NUTS
STARR FAMILY HOME STATE HISTORIC SITE

Historical Note:

Although Clara Willoughby's original recipe does not state in the original recipe, in a saucepan you should bring the water and sugar to a boil over medium to high heat, remove from heat and stir in nuts and orange zest, and spread on a baking sheet to cool.

INGREDIENTS:

2 C. nuts
½ C. water
2 C. sugar
Grated peel of orange

PROCESS:

When starts to thicken stir in nuts, stir continuously.

PECAN CANDY
MAGOFFIN HOME STATE HISTORIC SITE

Historical Note:

Candied pecans make a wonderful treat for the holidays. Octavia Magoffin would have kept sweets like these on hand for the family as they decorated their home or sat by the fire reading.

INGREDIENTS:

1½ lb. granulated sugar
1 C. water
1 lb. shelled pecans
Cinnamon

PROCESS:

Boil sugar and water until it forms ropy* from a spoon; then put in pecans and stir off of the fire until it becomes white. Grease a platter with butter, spread the candy, and put on it a sprinkle of cinnamon. When cold, break into pieces.

*'Ropy' is a term used to describe stringy threads.

ROSETTE IRON WAFERS
VARNER-HOGG PLANTATION STATE HISTORIC SITE

Historical Note:

Rosette iron wafers were a favorite of Ima Hogg. This recipe was taken from the lid of the box containing a rosette iron which had been purchased from Alfred Andresen & Co., Home Baking Department, Minneapolis, Minnesota.

INGREDIENTS:

2 eggs
1 tsp. sugar
½ tsp. salt
1 C. milk
1 C. flour (a little more if necessary)

NOTE:

Ifs and don'ts about making rosettes: If rosettes don't come off easily from the iron - they are not fried long enough to be dry in the center. If rosettes have several blisters that absorb the fat - eggs are beaten too much; beat but very little. If rosettes drop off into the oil or grease from iron - the iron is too hot. If batter slips off from the iron into the bowl - iron is not deep enough in the oil. If rosette is not crisp - it has been fried too quick.

PROCESS:

Beat eggs slightly with sugar and salt; add milk and flour, beat until smooth. This amount will make 40 rosettes. If wanted for oyster patties, or instead of toast, leave the sugar out of the batter. Screw handle into one of the irons and put Rosette Iron in hot lard or oil to heat before dipping it into the batter, not letting the batter come over the top of the iron. Return it to the hot lard, thoroughly covering the iron with same, for at least 20 seconds. Remove from iron with a piece of clean cheese cloth.

RICE PUDDING WITHOUT EGG
WASHINGTON-ON-THE-BRAZOS STATE HISTORIC SITE

Historical Note:

This *recipe was adapted from* ***The Indian Meal Book****, Eliza Leslie, 1846.*

INGREDIENTS:

½ pt. of rice
1 qt. of rich milk
4 heaping tsp. of brown sugar
1 tsp. of powdered cinnamon

PROCESS:

Rinse the rice thoroughly, draining it afterwards till as dry as possible. Stir it into a deep dish containing 1 quart of milk. Add the sugar and ground cinnamon. Set the dish into the oven, and bake the pudding 3 hours. It may be eaten warm, but it is best cold. This is a very good pudding, and economical when eggs are scarce. Some fresh butter, stirred in just before it goes to the oven will improve the mixture.

Interpreter, Laura Fisher, conducting campfire cooking at Barrington Living History Farm State Historic Site, Washington, Texas.

SÄCHSISCHER OSTERKUCHEN (SAXON EASTER CAKE)

KREISCHE BREWERY STATE HISTORIC SITE

Historical Note:

This rich, custardy cake comes from the German region of Saxony from where Heinrich Kreische immigrated in 1848. Each family had its own variation that was passed down through the generations.

CAKE INGREDIENTS:

2 C. flour
9 T. butter
1 packet(7 grams) vanilla sugar or extract
6 T. sugar
1 pinch salt
1 egg

PROCESS:

Preheat the oven to 350 degrees. For the dough: Mix the flour with the butter, vanilla, sugar, salt, and one egg, and knead into a dough. Cover the dough and allow it to rest at room temperature or warm oven for 30 minutes

FILLING INGREDIENTS:

2 C. quark (can substitute Greek yogurt)
4 egg yolks
1 C. sugar
2 T. brandy or rum
3 T. melted butter
1 small pinch saffron powder
½ C. ground almonds
½ C. currants
Zest of 1 lemon
4 oz. whipping cream
Flour for rolling

PROCESS:

For the filling: Drain the quark in a colander. Beat the egg yolks with the sugar, alcohol, melted butter, and saffron until the mixture is creamy and the sugar has completely dissolved. Stir in the almonds, followed by the currants, lemon zest, and cream. Stir in the quark as well. Spread out two thirds of the shortbread dough on a floured work surface. Place on the bottom of a greased springform pan (10"). Use the remaining third of the dough to form the sides. Spread the quark mixture in the spring form pan and smooth it out slightly. Bake at 350°F for about 50 minutes.

OPTIONAL TOPPING INGREDIENTS:

1 egg yolk
Water
Powdered sugar for dusting
Whipped cream

SAFFRON

PROCESS:

Mix the egg yolk with a little water. Remove the cake from the oven and drizzle the egg and water evenly over the surface of the cake. Return to the oven and allow the cake to bake for another 10-15 minutes. Remove the cake and allow to rest in the pan on a wire rack for 20 minutes. With a sharp knife, loosen the sides from the pan and remove the cake. Dust the cake with powdered sugar and serve while still warm, with whipped cream, if desired.

SUGARLESS CAKE
NATIONAL MUSEUM OF THE PACIFIC WAR STATE HISTORIC SITE

Historical Note:

This *recipe is from* **Recipes For Today**, *published by General Food Corporation, 1943.*

INGREDIENTS:

3 C. sifted cake flour
4 tsp. baking powder
½ tsp. salt
½ C. shortening
1½ C. corn syrup
3 egg yolks
2 tsp. grated orange rind
1 C. milk
3 egg whites

PROCESS:

Sift the flour, baking powder, and salt together. Stir shortening until creamy and add one cup of the corn syrup slowly until it becomes fluffy. Add egg yolks and beat well. Take turns alternating adding the dry ingredients and milk, stirring between each addition, then add the orange rind.

Beat the egg whites until stiff and add to the rest of the corn syrup gradually, beating until there are still peaks. Fold the batter until completely mixed. Bake in a greased cake pan at about 375 degrees for 25-30 minutes.

THE NUTMEG.

SWEET POTATO PIE
LEVI JORDAN PLANTATION STATE HISTORIC SITE

Historical Note:

This *recipe was adapted from* **The Southern Gardener and Receipt Book**, *P. Thornton, 1845.*

INGREDIENTS:

1-2 small lemons
4 large sweet potatoes
1 C. sugar
Allspice
Cinnamon
Butter
⅓ C. water
Pie dough to make a double-crust pie

PROCESS:

Slice the lemon(s) into very thin slices, leaving the peel on them. Wash and peel the sweet potatoes, slice them into very thin rounds. Line a pie pan with a bottom crust and begin to layer the sweet potato rounds arranged in circles within the pan. When the first layer of sweet potato is finished sprinkle it liberally with sugar, allspice, and cinnamon. Place thin slices of butter on top of the spices, followed by thin lemon slices placed evenly around the layer. Continue layering the pan with sweet potatoes, sugar, spices, butter, and lemon slices until it is full, finishing off with a layer of sweet potatoes, sugar, spices, and butter. Pour ⅓ cup water evenly over the layered ingredients Place the top crust, trim and crimp the edges. Make four to six cuts in the top crust to release steam. Bake at 400 degrees for one hour.

Interpreter, Chandler Wahrmund, serving drinks at Fanthorp Inn State Historic Site, Anderson, Texas.

BEVERAGES

CINCPAC SPECIAL

NATIONAL MUSEUM OF THE PACIFIC WAR STATE HISTORIC SITE

Historical Note:

The recipe was developed by Admiral Nimitz when he was Commander-in-Chief of the Pacific during World War II. At the time, liquor was rationed, a bottle a week to a man, and frequently, rum was the only kind available.

INGREDIENTS:

1 clean one-gallon jug
3 qts. bourbon
¼ of a fifth of gold-label rum
Sugar syrup
Tap water
2 whole vanilla beans, optional

PROCESS:

Add bourbon and gold-label rum to the one-gallon jug. Add sugar syrup until you can just detect the presence of sugar. Fill the remainder of the jug with tap water. Desirable but not necessary; drop two whole vanilla beans into the jug to stay for many refills of the jug. Pour generous portions over ice and serve it forth!

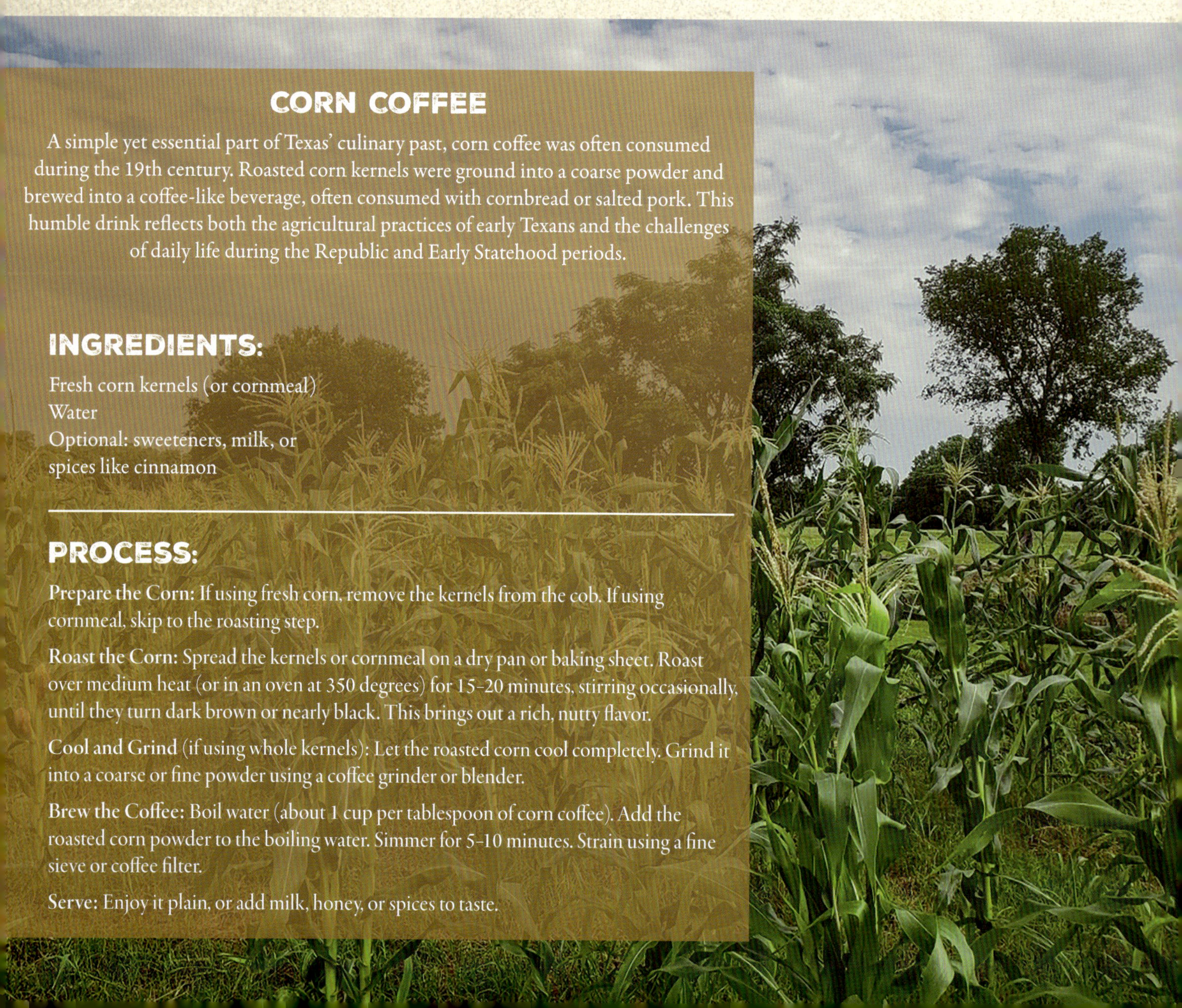

CORN COFFEE

A simple yet essential part of Texas' culinary past, corn coffee was often consumed during the 19th century. Roasted corn kernels were ground into a coarse powder and brewed into a coffee-like beverage, often consumed with cornbread or salted pork. This humble drink reflects both the agricultural practices of early Texans and the challenges of daily life during the Republic and Early Statehood periods.

INGREDIENTS:

Fresh corn kernels (or cornmeal)
Water
Optional: sweeteners, milk, or spices like cinnamon

PROCESS:

Prepare the Corn: If using fresh corn, remove the kernels from the cob. If using cornmeal, skip to the roasting step.

Roast the Corn: Spread the kernels or cornmeal on a dry pan or baking sheet. Roast over medium heat (or in an oven at 350 degrees) for 15-20 minutes, stirring occasionally, until they turn dark brown or nearly black. This brings out a rich, nutty flavor.

Cool and Grind (if using whole kernels): Let the roasted corn cool completely. Grind it into a coarse or fine powder using a coffee grinder or blender.

Brew the Coffee: Boil water (about 1 cup per tablespoon of corn coffee). Add the roasted corn powder to the boiling water. Simmer for 5-10 minutes. Strain using a fine sieve or coffee filter.

Serve: Enjoy it plain, or add milk, honey, or spices to taste.

COFFEE
FANTHORP INN STATE HISTORIC SITE

"Texas Molasses, Coffee, I am getting used to their coffee here [it] would suit Uncle Taylor first rate, it is so strong you could not sink an iron wedge in it without a crowbar, but now we have milk [so] I can go the coffee."

Abel Bearsley, long-term Fanthorp guest

COLD BREW COFFEE PROCESS:

Put a sufficient quantity of ground coffee into the percolator, placing it between the two strainers. Then (having stopped up the spout) pour into the upper strainer a due proportion of cold water; allowing a quart of water to half a pint or more of ground coffee. Cold water is now found to make a stronger infusion than hot water, as there is less evaporation, and none of the strength of the coffee is carried off in steam.

As soon as the water is all in, put on the lid closely, and set away the pot. It is well to put the coffee to infuse overnight, if wanted for breakfast; and in the morning, if required for evening. But, when necessary, it may be done in a much shorter time.

A little before the coffee is to go to table, lift off the upper half of the percolator, (the part that contains the strainers,) transfer the lid to the lower part; set the pot over the fire, and give it one boil up, not more.

As soon as it has come to a boil it is ready for drinking; being already strained, and drawn. It will be found clear, strong, and in all respects superior to that prepared in any other manner. A short boil is enough to take off any taste of rawness. Long boiling weakens coffee, and frequently lets it go bitter.

*Source: **Miss Leslie's New Receipts for Cookery,** Eliza Leslie, 1854.*

HOT COFFEE PROCESS:

Put two ounces of ground coffee into a stewpan or pot, which set upon the fire, stirring the powder round with a spoon until quite hot; then pour over a pint of boiling water; cover closely for five minutes, and pass it through a cloth ; warm it again, and serve hot.

The cloth through which the coffee is passed should be immediately washed and dried for the next occasion. This method has one great advantage, in the shortness of time necessary to obtain a cup of coffee.

*Source: **The American Matron-Practical and Scientific Cookery**, A. Housekeeper,1851.*

Interpreter, Chandler Wahrmund, conducting a coffee demonstration at Fanthorp Inn State Historic Site, Anderson, Texas.

COCKTAILS

MONUMENT HILL STATE HISTORIC SITE

After being released from Perote Prison in Vera Cruz, Mexico in 1844, the Mier Expedition survivors sailed back to Texas via New Orleans. Thomas Jefferson Green recalled,

"...and as we required neither clearance or porters, we wended our way up town, and called into the first open 'drinkery.' The Sherry Cobbler, a Tom & Jerry, and a Hail Storm, among the preferred beverages! These very men, I among the rest, who a few short weeks before, would have given a pint of their blood for a gill of the most miserable brandy ever distilled, now want, one a 'Sherry Cobbler', one a 'Tom & Jerry', and another a 'Hail Storm:' and all concluded that a little rose water round the edge of the cut glass would make it go the better."

SHERRY COBBLER

INGREDIENTS:

2 or 3 orange slices
½ oz. simple syrup
3½ oz. amontillado sherry
Mint
Seasonal berries

PROCESS:

Add oranges and simple syrup to mixing glass, then muddle. Add sherry and ice and shake. Strain into an ice filled glass. Garnish with orange, mint, add seasonal berries.

TOM & JERRY

INGREDIENTS:

1 oz. dark Jamaican rum
1 oz. cognac
1 T. Tom & Jerry Batter*
Hot milk or water
Ground nutmeg

PROCESS:

Add rum, cognac, and batter to a warm mug. Stir and top with hot milk or water. Garnish with nutmeg.

BATTER INGREDIENTS:

3 egg yolks and whites, separated
¼ tsp. cream of tartar
1 C. sugar
½ oz. rum
½ tsp. cinnamon
½ tsp. ground cloves
½ tsp. allspice

PROCESS:

Separate 3 egg yolks and whites. Whip egg whites with cream of tartar until stiff peaks form. In a separate bowl, beat yolks with the sugar, rum, cinnamon, ground cloves, and allspice. Gently fold yolk mixture into egg white mixture. Keep refrigerated or freeze.

HAIL STORM (MINT JULEP)

INGREDIENTS:

Fresh mint
¼ oz. simple syrup or even gin
2 oz. bourbon, rye, cognac, rum

PROCESS:

In a mixing glass, lightly muddle about 8 mint leaves with simple syrup. Add the spirit of choice and pack the glass tightly with ice. Stir until cup is frosted on the outside. Top with more crushed ice and garnish with a mint sprig.

During the 1800s, ice houses were used to store blocks of ice. The ice blocks were cut from frozen rivers and lakes and then transported to the ice houses. The ice houses were built to include gravel floors. Stone walls and straw were used to insulate the building. Ice blocks could be stored for many months and delivered as needed. It was expensive to purchase.

MARY MOODY'S HOLIDAY EGGNOG

LEVI JORDAN PLANTATION STATE HISTORIC SITE

INGREDIENTS:

3 egg yolks
4 rounded T. sugar
½ pt. whiskey
1 pint of cream

PROCESS:

Beat the egg yolks and sugar together until very thick. Slowly add ½ pint whiskey and fold in lightly (Old McCaskey's Whiskey is good or any other straight whiskey, but not a blended whiskey). Whip the cream very stiff. The cream should be measured before it is whipped. Gently fold whipped cream into the egg, sugar, and whiskey mixture.

NOTE

Consuming uncooked or unpasteurized eggs is now considered dangerous. Please make this with liquid egg yolks and whites from purchased cartons or pasteurized-in-the-shell eggs for health safety.

Left: Study room at Fulton Mansion State Historic Site, Fulton-Rockport, Texas.

PARTY PUNCH

MAGOFFIN HOME STATE HISTORIC SITE

Historical Note:

The Magoffins entertained many people in their home over the years and served punches like this during their annual New Year's Day open house. This citrusy punch was sure to have been a crowd pleaser.

INGREDIENTS:

2 qt. water
1 qt. sugar
Grated zest from 3 oranges
Grated zest from 3 lemons
Juice of two dozen oranges
Juice of 6 lemons
2 qt. sparkling water

PROCESS:

Boil together to a syrup two quarts water and one quart sugar. Grate zest from three oranges and three lemons and put in syrup overnight. Add the juice of two dozen oranges and six lemons and strain the mixture. Add two quarts sparkling water. You may add whiskey, rum, or any wine to suit your taste. For a large party, a stack of strong tea is also good.

ICED TEA

SAM BELL MAXEY STATE HISTORIC SITE

Historical Note:

Many late 19th and early 20th century cookbooks contain recipes for everyday things we tend to make intuitively today. But sometimes the "official" cookbook versions are made a little differently, as in this recipe from Fanny Farmer's Boston Cooking School Cook Book. Recipe adapted from ***The Boston Cooking School Cook Book****, Fannie Farmer, 1915 edition.*

INGREDIENTS:

4 tsp. loose tea
2 C. boiling water
Cracked ice
Sugar to taste
1 lemon, sliced

PROCESS:

Scald or heat an earthenware or china teapot to warm it. Put in 4 teaspoons of loose tea and pour in the boiling water. Cover and let stand in a warm location for five minutes. Strain the brewed tea into glasses one-third full of cracked ice. Sweeten to taste and allow one slice of lemon per glass.

The flavor is much finer by chilling the infusion quickly. Avoid a second steeping of leaves, even with the addition of some fresh ones as so large an amount of tannins will be extracted that will make the second glasses taste bitter.

TRADITIONAL EGGNOG

SAM BELL MAXEY HOUSE STATE HISTORIC SITE

Historical Note:

Eggnog recipes can be found globally, with only slight variances in their ingredients. In Spain, 'Rompon' or 'Ponche de Huevo' and in France, 'Lait de Poule' are similar to the English recipes. In the Dominican Republic, 'Ponche Crema de Ron' calls for condensed milk and rum, while recipes called Eierlikor in Germany use brandy. Sam and Lala Long, the Maxey's adopted son and his wife, hosted many parties and served eggnog at their holiday gatherings.

INGREDIENTS:

2 eggs, separated
2 T. sugar
2 oz. bourbon
½ pt. whipping cream, whipped
Ground nutmeg

PROCESS:

Beat egg yolks until thick. Add sugar and bourbon. Fold in whipped cream and then stiffly beaten egg whites. Serve eggnog very cold with a sprinkle of freshly ground nutmeg. Serves four.

NOTE

Consuming uncooked or unpasteurized eggs is now considered dangerous. Please make this with liquid egg yolks and whites from purchased cartons or pasteurized-in-the-shell eggs for health safety.

MEASURING UP: HOW FANNY FARMER HELPED HOME COOKS

Fanny Farmer was a major figure in American cooking who helped transform how people prepared and understood food. Born in 1857, she faced serious health problems in her youth but eventually enrolled at the Boston Cooking School. She later became the school's principal, where she influenced many students and home cooks.

In 1896, Farmer published *The Boston Cooking-School Cook Book*, which became one of the most widely used cookbooks in the country. What set her book apart was its clear, detailed instructions and the use of standardized measurements. This made recipes easier to follow and more consistent, especially for people cooking at home.

Farmer's cookbook was revolutionary for its time. Earlier cookbooks often gave vague directions, but hers offered tested recipes with exact amounts. She also included advice on nutrition and explained some of the science behind cooking. Her work helped make cooking a more respected and structured subject, and it shaped the way modern recipes are written today.

Bits and Bobs

COLD CREAM FOR A SMOOTH COMPLEXION

Historical Note:

Recipe redacted from ***The New Home Cook Book***, The Ladies of Chicago Et. Al., 1911.

INGREDIENTS:

4 oz. of almond oil
2 oz. of rosewater
2 oz. of white wax
2 oz. of cocoa butter
2 oz. of jojoba oil

PROCESS:

Place a bowl in a pan of boiling water; cut the white wax and cocoa butter in small pieces; put them in the bowl, also the almond oil and rose water. When melted, stir contents until cold.

A Double Boiler.

CURRY POWDER WASHINGTON-ON-THE-BRAZOS STATE HISTORIC SITE

Historical Note:

Often housewives and cooks made their own spice mixtures to use in specialized dishes. This curry powder is a good example of their concoctions. This recipe was adapted from ***The Housekeeper's Assistant****, Anna H. Allen, 1845.*

INGREDIENTS:

3 oz. of coriander seed
5 oz. of turmeric,
1 oz. of black pepper,
1 oz. of mustard-seed,
1 oz. of ginger,
1 oz. cayenne pepper,
1 oz. of lesser cardamom,
1 oz. of cinnamon,
1 oz. of cumin seed.

PROCESS:

Grind all the ingredients to a fine powder. Pass them through a mesh sieve and mix them well. Bottle the mixture into an airtight container and keep it in a dry dark place until use, and keep in a dry place. It will keep for up to one year.

The Spice Box - Has six separate boxes that take out, so that whole or ground spices may be kept nice and separate.

HOT SPICE

SAM BELL MAXEY HOUSE STATE HISTORIC SITE

Historical Note:

Delicious with pork chops, steaks, and gravies. This recipe was adapted from Mrs. Beeton's ***The Book of Household Management****, 1861.*

INGREDIENTS:

2 tsp. ground ginger
2 tsp. ground black pepper
2 tsp. ground cinnamon
7 garlic cloves, minced
1 oz. grated nutmeg
½ oz. mace
¼ oz. cayenne
1-½ oz. white pepper

PROCESS:

Pound the ingredients mix them thoroughly together. For a spicier mixture, increase the cayenne amount.

Stone Metate.

KITCHEN PEPPER

WASHINGTON-ON-THE-BRAZOS STATE HISTORIC SITE

Historical Note:

Recipes named 'Kitchen Pepper" are found in cookbooks as old as the mid-18th century and remain popular until at least the 1870s. This recipe was adapted from ***The Manuscript of Ann Maria Morris****, 1824.*

INGREDIENTS:

1 tsp. ground ginger
1 tsp. ground ceylon cinnamon
1 tsp. ground blackpepper
1 tsp. ground allspice
½ tsp. grated nutmeg
½ tsp. ground cloves
6 tsp. salt

PROCESS:

Mix all the spices together very well, being careful to ensure that all of the spices are evenly mixed. Store in a sealed jar or plastic baggie. Use in gravies, beef soups, or a rub on beef or pork roasts.

BLACK PEPPER.

Grinding spices during San Jacinto Battleground State Historic Site's Fall Fandango event in La Porte, Texas.

LIP SALVE FOR CHAPPED LIPS

Historical Note:

This recipe was adapted from ***The Dudley Book of Cookery and Household Recipes,*** *Georgina Elizabeth Ward, 1909*

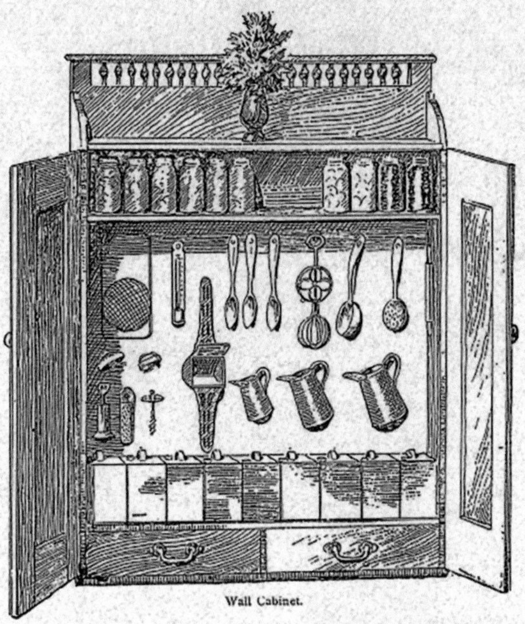

Wall Cabinet.

INGREDIENTS:

1 oz. of almond oil
.25 oz. of beeswax
3 drops of rose oil
.5 oz. of jojoba oil

PROCESS:

Melt the ingredients gradually and work well so as to make into a smooth stiff cream. Place it into small jars for use.

MUSHROOM POWDER

VARNER-HOGG PLANTATION STATE HISTORIC SITE

Historical Note:

This is a valuable addition to sauces and gravies when fresh mushrooms are not attainable. This recipe was adapted from ***Mrs. Beeton's The Book of Household Management****, 1861.*

INGREDIENTS:

½ peck of large mushrooms
2 onions, chopped finely
12 garlic cloves, chopped
¼ oz. dry mace
2 tsp. of white pepper

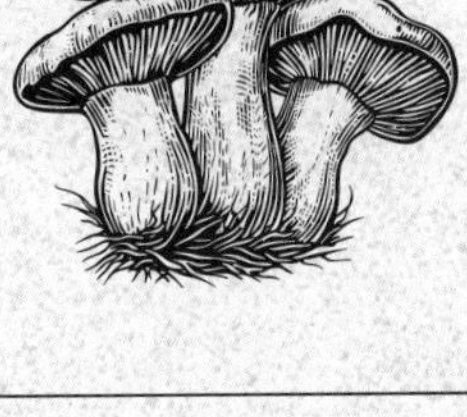

PROCESS:

Peel and wash the mushrooms. Put them into a stew pan with the rest of the ingredients without water. Sauté them over a clear fire until all liquid has evaporated. Be sure not to burn. Arrange all sautéed ingredients on a baking sheet and place them in a slow oven until all ingredients are dried. Once cooled, pound them into a fine powder. Be sure to store in dry bottles.

PREPARED MUSTARD

SAM BELL MAXEY HOUSE STATE HISTORIC SITE

Historical Note:

This recipe was adapted from ***The New Home Cook Book, The Ladies of Chicago*** *Et. Al., 1911.*

INGREDIENTS:

2 T. dry mustard powder
1 tsp. of sugar
½ tsp. of salt
Water
1 T. Salad oil
Vinegar

PROCESS:

Mix mustard powder, sugar, salt in enough boiling water to dissolve the ingredients. Add salad oil and enough vinegar to thin it. This should keep a week or two.

RASBERRY VINEGAR

SAM BELL MAXEY HOUSE STATE HISTORIC SITE

Historical Note:

This recipe was adapted from ***The New Home Cook Book, The Ladies of Chicago*** *Et. Al., 1911.*

INGREDIENTS:

2-4 qts. of red rasberries
Vinegar
1 lb. of sugar

PROCESS:

To four quarts red raspberries, put enough vinegar to cover, and let them stand 24 hours; scald and strain it; add a pound of sugar to one pint of juice; boil it 20 minutes, and bottle; it is then ready for use and will keep years.

VENISON OR BEEF JERKY

CHARLES AND MARY ANN GOODNIGHT RANCH STATE HISTORIC SITE

Historical Note:

Jerky was a staple on the frontier. Before refrigerators, drying meat was the only way to preserve it. It is an efficient protein source for cowboys while driving cattle and working on the ranch. This recipe was adapted from ***Legends of America: Traveling through American History, Destinations, and Legends.***

INGREDIENTS:

3 lbs. of fresh venison or beef
5 T. black pepper
4 T. allspice
Salt to taste

PROCESS:

Skin one thigh of the animal, muscle by muscle removing all the membranes so that only the raw and moist flesh remains. The best size meat is pieces about 1 foot long 6" wide, and 2 or 3 inches thick. Rub the spice mixture into the meat. Be sure to cover every bit of the meat's surface. Hang each piece by the small end to dry. If the sun is too hot, hang it in the shade. Never let the meat get wet or damp; take it inside if it rains. Cover the meat with canvas or cloth to protect it from the dew. This will be at its best at a month old.

BEEF.

A Bullock marked as cut into joints by the Butcher.

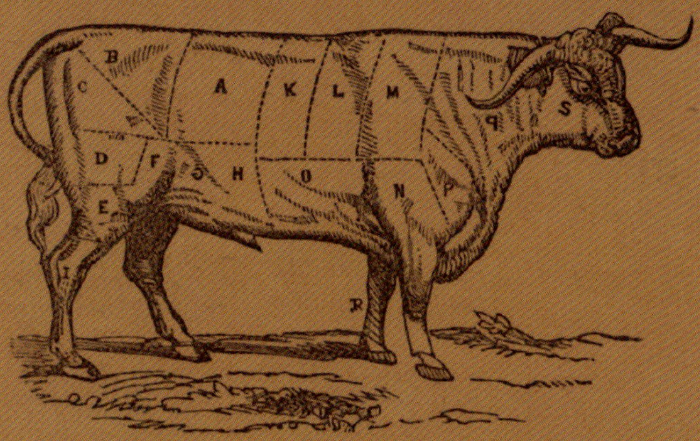

A Sirloin.
B Rump.
C Aitchbone.
D Buttock.
E Mouse Buttock.
F Veiny Piece.
G Thick Flank.
H Thin Flank.
I Leg.
K Fore Ribs, containing five ribs.
L Middle Rib, containing four ribs.
M Chuck Rib, containing three ribs.
N Shoulder, or leg of Mutton piece
O Brisket.
P Clod.
Q Neck, or Sticking Piece.
R Shin.
S Cheek.

The baron of beef is formed of the pieces marked A. B. united on both sides.

Conclusion

Your culinary tour of Texas history will hopefully have brought you a better understanding of the various cultures that have joined together across time to create the state cuisine we recognize today. Maybe it will give you pause to think about how your own family's cultural heritage and foodways reflect on your place within our shared history. Perhaps it will inspire you to cook more dishes from the past or explore new ways to approach how you prepare and present the foods that you make.

We hope that you have enjoyed taking your place at our Texas table!

APPENDICES

Historic Tables of Measurement Conversions

Table of Weights and Measures, for persons who have neither scales nor weights, ***Mrs. Chadwick's Home Cookery***, 1853.

1 lb. of wheat flour	**1 quart**
1 lb. 2 oz. of indian meal	**1 quart**
1 lb. of butter when soft	**1 quart**
1 lb. of broken loaf sugar, broken up	**1 quart**
1 lb. 1 oz. of powdered loaf sugar	**1 quart**
1 lb. 1 oz. of best brown sugar	**1 quart**
10 eggs	**1 pound**
1 tablespoon salt	**1 ounce**
16 large tablespoonfuls	**½ pint**
8 large tablespoonfuls	**1 gill**
4 large tablespoonfuls	**½ gill**

25 drops thin liquid	**1 teaspoon**
A common tumbler	**holds ½ pint, or 8 ounces**
A common wineglass	**holds ½ gill, or 4 large tablespoons 4 wineglasses equal ½ pint or 8 ounces**
A common teacup	**holds 6 ounces**
1 gallon	**8 pints**
1 pint	**16 ounces**
1 ounce	**8 drachms**
Half a gallon	**¼ peck**
One gallon	**half a peck**
Two gallons	**one peck**
Four gallons	**half a bushel**
Eight gallons	**one bushel**

Manual of Domestic Work-Practical Lesson in Cookery, Anna Woodbury, 1889.

One quart of flour	1 pound
One pint of granulated sugar	1 pound
Two cups of packed butter	1 pound
Ten eggs	1 pound
Two and a half cup of powdered sugar	1 pound
Four cups of flour	1 pound
Three cups of meal	1 pound
One heaping tablespoons of granulated sugar	1 ounce
Two full tablespoons of powdered sugar	1 ounce
One full table spoonful of butter	1 ounce
Two full tablespoons of flour	1 ounce
Two full tablespoons for coffee	1 ounce
One pint of chopped meat closely packed	1 pound

4 salt spoonsful	1 teaspoon
4 teaspoonfuls	1tablespoon
2 tablespoonfuls	1 ounce
4 tablespoonfuls	1 wine glass, or ½ a gill
8 tablespoonfuls	4 ounces make a gill
4 gills	1 pint
2 pints	1 quart

A Comparative Table of eights and Measures, from ***Science in e Kitchen: A Practical Explanation of Principles of Healthful Cookery***, Mrs. E. Kellogg, 1893.

1 heaping tablespoonful of sugar	1 ounce
2 rounded tablespoonfuls of white flour	1 ounce
2 cupfuls of granulated sugar	1 pound
2 cupfuls of meal	1 pound
4 cupfuls of sifted flour	1 pound
1 pint of oatmeal, cracked wheat, or other coarse grains	1 pound
1 pint of liquid	1 pound
1 pint of chopped or ground meat packed solid	1 pound
7 heaping tabelspoonfuls of sugar	1 cupful
5 heaping tablespoonfuls of flour	1 cupful
Two cupfuls of liquid or dry material	1 pint
4 cupfuls of liquid or dry material	1 quart

Determining the temperature of a main oven or bake kettle

A slow or slack oven	275-300 degrees
A moderate oven	325-375 degrees
A hot oven	400-425 degrees
A quick oven	450 degrees

To determine the temperature of an oven with no thermometer bake kettle, the following guideline may be helpful. If a hand is held near the cooking surface for 20-25 seconds, the oven is a quick oven, 25-35 seconds is a hot oven, 35-45 seconds is a moderate oven; and 45-60 seconds the oven is slow.

Chief of Interpretation, Hal Simon, and volunteer interpreters conducting foodways programming and enjoying a meal in the kitchen at the French Legation State Historic Site, Austin, Texas.

Coming to the Table: Historic Place Settings in America, 1850-1930

by Hal Simon
Chief of Interpretation
Texas Historical Commission

Contextualizing historic place settings enables researchers and those interested in the presentation of period cooking to consider how food was served, and tables were presented. Table settings revealed a lot about changes in the American approach to dining.

A place setting, often referred to as a "cover," consists of the plates, glasses, silver, and napkins to be used by each person. The covers on opposite sides of the table should be directly opposite each other, not out of line. Lay the covers, allowing 24 to 30 inches from plate to plate for formal meals. (Refer to figure diagram 1.1)

The fork is placed to the left of the plate, the knife above the plate (one assumes with the handle to the right), the napkin to the right of the plate, with the tumbler directly above the napkin but pretty much beside the plate rather than above it to the upper right-hand corner as often done today.

Another illustration from the same publication (diagram 1.2) described as the drawing of a tea-table. Small sized plates are set around, with only a knife. The position of the napkin, and tumbler are the same in her dinner diagram. The food items being served are placed symmetrically in the center of the table. On the waiter (tray) are placed the teacups and saucers, sugar bowl, slop bowl, cream cup, and two or three containers of tea, coffee, and water. Mrs. Beecher comments,

"This drawing may aid some housekeepers in teaching a domestic how to set a tea-table, as the picture will assist the memory in some cases."

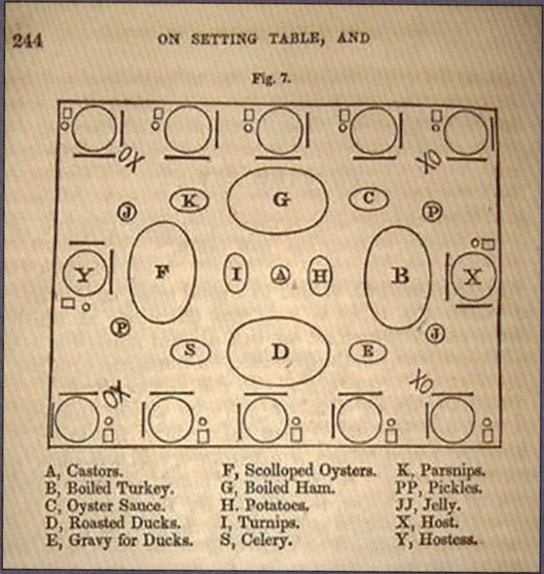

1.1 The first table setting diagram is from ***Mrs. Beecher's Domestic Receipt Book***, 1850.

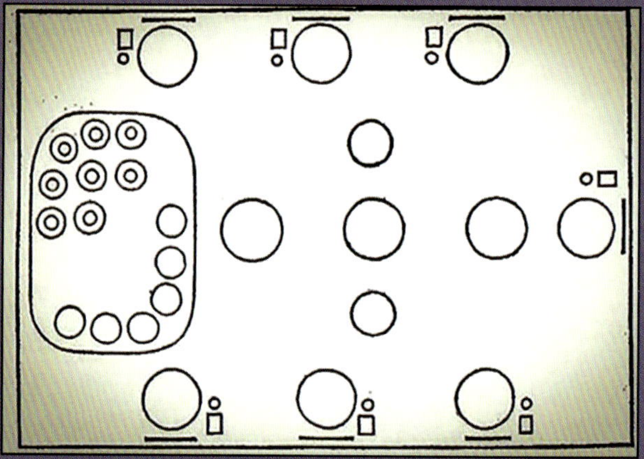

1.2 The table laid for teatime diagram from ***Mrs. Beecher's Domestic Receipt Book***, 1850.

1.3 ***Godey's Lady's Book***, March 1859. A table laid for dinner.

Table set for Serving from the Side.

1.4 Mary Foote Henderson's "***Practical Cooking and Dinner Giving***", 1877. A table laid for service a la Rus.

Nearly a decade later, ***Godey's Lady's Book***, March 1859, a dinner table example (Diagram 1.3) shows how the location of items in place settings changes ever so slightly across so many publications of the time, year by year. The fork and spoon are placed beside the plate, the knife is placed above the plate, and the napkin has moved from the right side to the left side. The fact that the napkins are shown in rings implies that this is a family meal, as napkin rings are only used to identify each individual's napkin in domestic settings when they will be reused for more than one meal.

There is a noticeable lack of wine glasses in both the 1850 and 1859 table diagrams shown below. That doesn't imply that wine was not being served, during this period wineglasses were brought to the table when each was appropriate, rather than being a part of the pre-set cover.

In Mary Foote Henderson's "Practical Cooking and Dinner Giving" 1877, this table setting diagram (1.4) appears, with a lengthy and fairly florid description, quoted below:

> In serving a dinner a la Russe, the table is decorated by placing the dessert in a tasteful manner around a centre-piece of flowers. This furnishes a happy mode of gratifying other senses than taste; for while the appetite is being satisfied, the flowers exhale their fragrance, and give the eye what never fails to please the refined and cultivated guest.
>
> In this style the dishes are brought to the table already carved, and ready for serving, thus depriving the cook of the power to display his decorative art, and the host his skill at carving. Each dish is served as a separate course, only one vegetable being allowed for a course, unless merely used for the purpose of garnishing.
>
> I will describe the "setting" or arranging of the table, which may be advantageously adopted. In the first place, a round table five feet in diameter is the best calculated to show off a dinner. If of this size, it may be decorated to great advantage, and conveniently used for six or eight persons, without enlargement.
>
> Put a thick baize under the table-cloth. This is quite indispensable. It prevents noise, and the finest and handsomest table-linen looks comparatively thin and sleazy on a bare table. Do not put starch in the napkins, as it renders them stiff and disagreeable, and only a very little in the table-cloth. They should be thick enough, and, at the same time, of fine enough texture, to have firmness without starch. Too much cannot be said as to the pleasant effect of a dinner, when the table-linen is of spotless purity, and the dishes and silver are perfectly bright.

Henderson also wrote:

"Although many ornaments may be used in decorating the table, yet nothing is so pretty and so indicative of a refined taste as flowers. If you have no epergne for them, use a compotier or raised dish, with a plate upon the top, to hold cut flowers; or place flower-pots with blossoming plants on the table. A network of wire painted green, or of wood or crochet work, may be used to conceal the roughness of the flowerpot. A still prettier arrangement is to set the pot in a jardinière vase."

"At a dinner party, place a little bouquet by the side of the plate of each lady, in a small glass or silver bouquet - holder. At the gentlemen's, plates put a little bunch of three or four flowers, called a boutonniere, in the folds of the napkin. As soon as the gentlemen are seated at table, they may attach them to the left lapel of the coat.

"Place the dessert in two or four fancy dessert - dishes around the centre-piece, which, by-the-way, should not be high enough to obstruct the view of persons sitting at opposite sides of the table. The dessert will consist of fruits, fresh or candied, preserved ginger, or preserves of any kind, fancy cakes, candies, nuts, raisins, etc.

"Put as many knives, forks, and spoons by the side of the plate of each person as will be necessary to use in all the different courses. Place the knives and spoons on the right side, and the forks on the left side, of the plates. This saves the trouble of replacing a knife and fork or spoon as each course is brought on. Many prefer the latter arrangement, as they object to the appearance of so many knives, etc., by the sides of a plate. This is, of course, a matter of taste. I concede the preferable appearance of the latter plan, but confess a great liking for any arrangement which saves extra work and confusion.

"Place the napkin, neatly folded, on the plate, with a piece of bread an inch thick, and three inches long, or a small cold bread roll, in the folds or on the top of the napkin.

"Put a glass for water, and as many wine-glasses as are necessary at each plate. Fill the water-glass just before the dinner is announced, unless carafes are used. These are kept on the table all the time, well filled with water, one carafe being sufficient for two or three persons. All the wine intended to be served decanted should be placed on the table, conveniently arranged at different points.

"At opposite sides of the table place salt and pepper stands, together with the different fancy spoons, crossed by their side, which may be necessary at private dinners, for serving dishes.

"Select as many plates as will be necessary for all the different courses. Those intended for cold dishes, such as salad, dessert, etc., place on the sideboard, or at any convenient place. Have those plates intended for dessert already prepared, with a finger-bowl on each plate. The finger-glasses should be half filled with water, with a slice of lemon in each, or a geranium leaf and one flower, or a little boutonniere: a sprig of lemon verbena is pretty, and leaves a pleasant odor on the fingers after pressing it in the bowl. In Paris, the water is generally warm, and scented with peppermint.

"Some place folded fruit -napkins under each finger-bowl; others have little fancy net -work mats, made of thread or crochet cotton, which are intended to protect handsome painted dessert-plates from scratches which the finger-bowls might possibly make.

"This is little enough every-day ceremony for families of the most moderate pretensions, and it is also enough for the finest dinner party, with the simple addition of more waiters, and distribution of the work among them. It is well that this simple ceremony should be daily observed."

In the same 1877 book, Mary Foot Henderson also describes serving dinner a la Anglais, shown in diagram 1.5. Her description of serving a la Anglais, in much shorter and more dismissive terms, says,

"The English mode is to set the whole of each course, often containing many dishes, at once upon the table. Such dishes as require carving, after having been once placed on the dinner table, are removed to a side-table, and there carved by an expert servant. Serving several dishes at one time, of course, impairs the quality of many, on account of the impossibility of keeping them hot. This might, in fact, render some dishes quite worthless."

Mrs. Henderson also outlines some other very pithy directions, having to do with dinner service. Her statements reflect a strong preference for Service a la Russe, which required a great deal more domestic staff.

- **Never overload or over supply a table. It is a vulgar hospitality.**
- **When you invite a person to a family dinner, do not attempt too much. It is really more elegant to have the dinner appear as if it were an everyday affair.**
- **Many Americans are deterred from entertaining, because they do not think they can have company without a vulgar abundance, which is an expensive and troublesome as it is coarse and unrefined.**
- **Care must be taken about when selecting company for a dinner party. Always put the question to yourself, "Why do I ask him or her?". Unless the answer be satisfactory, leave him or her out."**

In the 1888 book, ***Mrs. Corson's Practical Cookery and Household Management***, the table set with dinner covers for multiple guests and differs very little from Mary Foote Henderson's table laid for service a la Anglais. She recommended the laying of multiple pieces of silverware, *"as many wineglasses as are necessary,"* the salt cellar and pepper stand/shaker at the corner, napkin folded at each place setting with a piece of bread/bread roll inside of it, and at least one carafe/ decanter. She shows shades being used on the candles, to reduce the glare of their flames.

Table set for Serving on the Table.

1.5 Mary Foote Henderson's, ***Practical Cooking and Dinner Giving***, 1877 . A table laid for service a la Anglais.

Mrs. Corson's Practical Cookery and Household Management makes several different observations about laying the table. She noted that tablecloths should be laid without any creases or folds in it, that is has become fashionable to lay a strip of bright colored plush or satin down the middle of the table, or that a wide piece of very open lace with a definite pattern laid over a matching piece of satin, silk, or cambric is also appropriate.

She also stated that large caster sets had gone out of favor and are not even found on sideboard in usual circumstances, and that butter, when it is served, often has a small plate and special knife placed for use. ***"The disuse of butter is traced to countries where it is less plentiful than in America,"*** and that she hopes the current trend does not continue.

Mrs. Corson's ***Practical Cookery and Household Management***, 1885.
Service a la Anglais

In the 20th century, publications with illustrations showed standards and preferences for formal place settings.

For a formal table service, Mrs. Allen states in her 1916 book ***Table Service***, that,

"Mark the position of the covers by laying the service or place plates, which should be not less than ten inches in diameter. Lay the covers, allowing twenty-four to thirty inches from plate to plate.

In laying a bare table, the covers are marked by the plate doilies. A service plate is laid for each person, one inch from the edge of the table; this plate remains upon the table until it is necessary to replace it with a hot plate.

Next, lay the silver, which should always be placed in the order in which it is to be used, beginning at the outside and using toward the plate.

Silver for the dessert course is never put on with the silver required for the other courses, except for the dinner which is served without a maid, when everything should be done to avoid the necessity of leaving the table. Neither is the table set with more than three forks. If more are required, they are placed with their respective courses."

Formal Table Cover from ***Table Service***, Lucy Grace Allen, 1916, page 27.

For a table laid for a home dinner when a maid of staff is not available for serving, Lucy Grace Allen says in her 1916 book, ***Table Service***,

"Place the napkin, preferably flat and squarely folded, at the left of the forks. The hem and selvage of the napkin should be parallel with the forks and the edge of the table, this position bringing the embroidered letter, if there be one, in the right place. Napkins are sometimes given additional folds to save space.

Place the water glass at the point of the knife; the bread-and-butter plate above the service plate, a little to the left; and the butter spreader across the upper, right-hand side of the bread-and-butter plate, with the blade turned toward the center of the plate.

At first-class hotels, the butter spreader is often found at the right with the other knives, but this is not consistent with home table service."

Little changed between the 1915 and 1930 diagrams, and things continued to move toward more informality and self-expression in the table settings.

Looking back at how the food was and tables were presented in the past can spark an interest in social customs, and expand your Foodways knowledge beyond food preparation, to its presentation and how individuals were expected to eat in various formal and informal settings. The examples presented here illustrate our complex relationship with food and dining for and may help spark good conversations about cultural change over time.

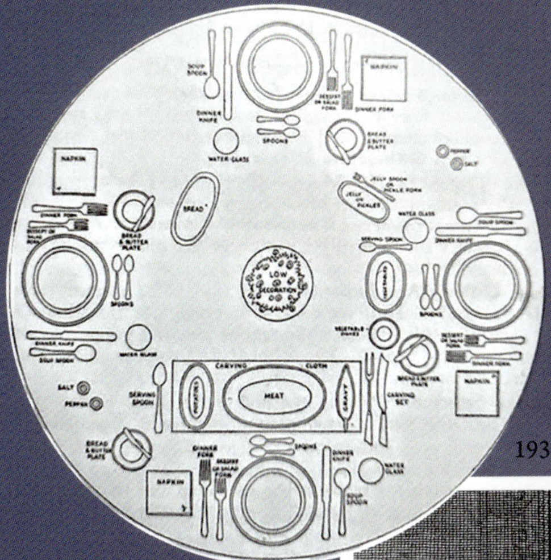

1930, for Service a la Anglais

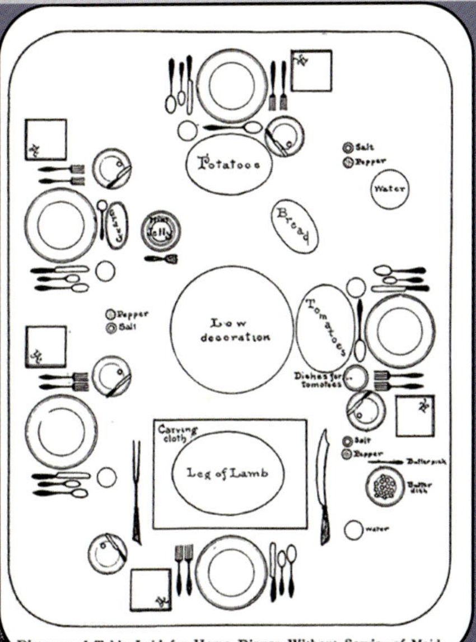

Diagram of Table Laid for Home Dinner Without Service of Maid.

Table Laid for Home Dinner Without Service of Maid, from ***Table Service***, Lucy Grace Allen, 1916, page 60

OUR 42 STATE HISTORIC SITES

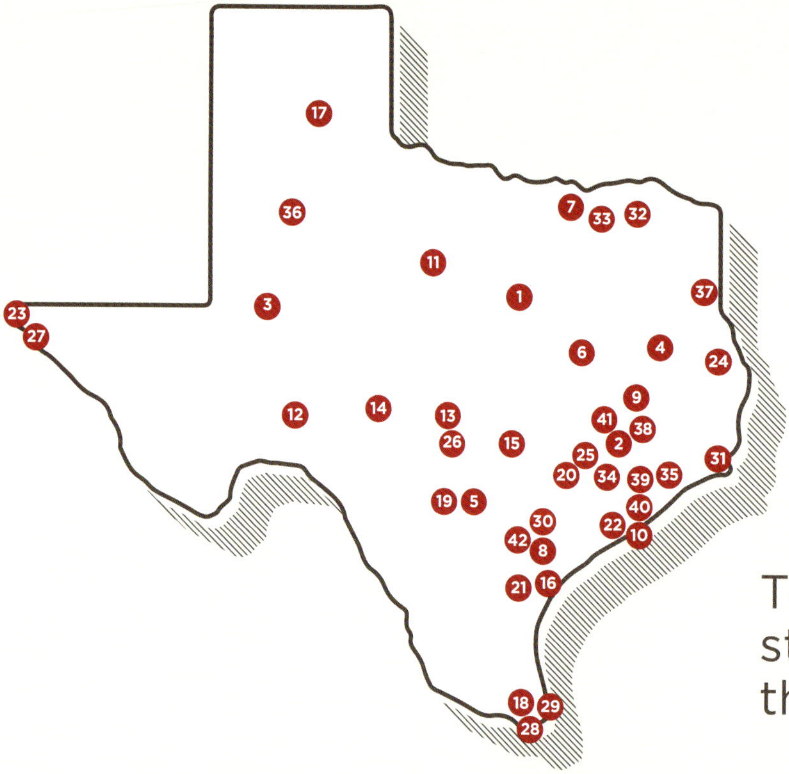

1. Acton
2. Barrington Living History Farm
3. Bush Family Home
4. Caddo Mounds
5. Casa Navarro
6. Confederate Reunion Grounds
7. Eisenhower Birthplace
8. Fannin Battleground
9. Fanthorp Inn
10. First Capitol of Texas
11. Fort Griffin
12. Fort Lancaster and Battlefield
13. Fort Martin Scott
14. Fort McKavett
15. French Legation
16. Fulton Mansion
17. Goodnight Ranch
18. Iwo Jima Museum and Monument
19. Kreische Brewery
20. Landmark Inn
21. Levi Jordan Plantation
22. Lipantitlán
23. Magoffin Home
24. Mission Dolores
25. Monument Hill
26. National Museum of the Pacific War
27. Old Socorro Mission
28. Palmito Ranch Battlefield
29. Port Isabel Lighthouse
30. Presidio La Bahía
31. Sabine Pass Battleground
32. Sam Bell Maxey House
33. Sam Rayburn House
34. San Felipe de Austin
35. San Jacinto Battleground and Museum
36. Slaton Harvey House
37. Star of the Republic Museum
38. Starr Family Home
39. Stephen F. Austin Memorial
40. Varner-Hogg Plantation
41. Washington-on-the-Brazos
42. Zaragoza Birthplace

Telling the story of Texas through the ages

Acton State Historic Site
FM 167, Acton, TX 76049
In the small town of Acton, five miles outside of Granbury, a statue of Elizabeth Crockett appears to be looking for her husband in the distance. Towering over Acton Cemetery, this regal monument marks the burial site of Davy Crockett's second wife, Elizabeth, who died in 1860 at the age of 72. and pays tribute to the widow of one of the nation's most celebrated folk heroes.

Bush Family Home State Historic Site
400 E. Broadway, Midland, TX 79701
The Bush Family Home is listed in the National Register of Historic Places as the residence of an exceptional political family who shaped state and national politics in the late 20th and early 21st centuries. This home has been restored to the early 1950s and reflects the lives of the young family through exhibits and furnishings.

Barrington Living History Farm State Historic Site
23100 Barrington Lane, Washington, TX 77880
Travel back in time to 1850 and explore the original home of Dr. Anson Jones, the last President of the Republic of Texas. The Jones family lived at the farm for over a decade, building a successful cotton farm with enslaved labor after Texas joined the union. This living history farm is complete with period costumed interpreters using 19th century farming practices for planting, cultivating, harvesting, and working with livestock. Explore the sights and smells of farm life and experience the daily lives of those who came 150 years ago.

Caddo Mounds State Historic Site
1649 State Hwy. 21 West, Alto, TX 75925
More than 1,200 years ago, a group of ancestral Caddo built a village and ceremonial center here. Today, three earthen mounds, still considered sacred to Caddo people, rise from the lush Piney Woods landscape. Learn how the Caddo lived on the land through immersive museum exhibits and programs.

Casa Navarro State Historic Site
228 S. Laredo Street, San Antonio, TX 78207
A rancher, merchant, and one of only two native-born Texans to sign the Texas Declaration of Independence, José Antonio Navarro was a leading advocate for Tejano rights. Casa Navarro State Historic Site celebrates his life at his original 1850s adobe and limestone home, a historic jewel among its urban surroundings.

Charles and Mary Ann Goodnight Ranch State Historic Site
2000 US Hwy. 287, Goodnight, TX 79226
Charles Goodnight co-founded the JA Ranch in 1876, the first cattle ranch in the Texas Panhandle. In 1887, he built a Victorian home for his new venture, the Goodnight-Thayer Cattle Company. His wife Mary Ann helped run the ranch and preserve American bison. Today, the restored home features a spacious second-floor porch overlooking descendants of the Goodnights' original bison herd.

Confederate Reunion Grounds State Historic Site
1738 FM 2705, Mexia, TX 76667
On the edge of the Navasota River, Confederate Reunion Grounds State Historic Site commemorates a place where Confederate Civil War veterans and families reunited from 1889–1946. Today, it remains a gathering place for events and family reunions, and features a 1902 dance pavilion, Civil War-era cannon, and ruins of structures from the "Roaring '20s" and Mexia Oil Boom.

Eisenhower Birthplace State Historic Site
609 S. Lamar Avenue, Denison, TX 75021
The Eisenhower Birthplace State Historic Site showcases the home where the 34th U.S. President Dwight David "Ike" Eisenhower was born in 1890. Antique furnishings fill the modest frame house, illustrating the working-class life of the Eisenhowers. The visitor center celebrates Ike with memorabilia and exhibits featuring his many accomplishments as president and war hero.

Fannin Battleground State Historic Site
734 FM 2506, Fannin, TX 77960
After Col. James W. Fannin surrendered to Mexican forces at this site, Gen. Santa Anna ordered him and his men executed in nearby Goliad, against the wishes of other Mexican commanders. The surrender, and unanticipated execution, inflamed the Texas cause, spurring the battle cry "Remember Goliad!"

Fanthorp Inn State Historic Site
579 S. Main Street, Anderson, TX 77830
Fanthorp Inn began as a two-room cedar log dogtrot cabin in 1834, when Texas was still part of Mexico. By 1850 it grew to the 17 room complex you can see today. English immigrant, Henry Fanthorp petitioned Stephen F. Austin for permission to settle in Austin's colony upon his arrival to Texas in 1832. He bought 1,100 acres and built his house in 1834 on the road that crossed his land, thus bringing travelers to his door immediately. Within time, Fanthorp's Inn became a well-known stopping place for both travelers and the community.

First Capitol of Texas State Historic Site
200 N. 14th St. West Columbia, TX 77486
Columbia (now West Columbia) was the capital of Texas on October 22, 1836. On that day, Sam Houston, the first president of the new Texas Republic, gave his inaugural address on the steps of the original Capitol. The inauguration had been scheduled for December, but ad interim president David Burnet resigned unexpectedly, leaving Houston just two hours to prepare his speech. This site will be developed as the home to a replica of the original Capitol building and a park with a path connecting a series of monuments that commemorate the history of this area.

Fort Griffin State Historic Site
1701 N. U.S. Hwy. 283, Albany, TX 76430
Remnants of the fort remain today at Fort Griffin State Historic Site, which is also home to the Official State of Texas Longhorn Herd and offers camping, hiking, stargazing, and living history. Fort Griffin is a State Archeological Landmark and listed in the National Register of Historic Places.

Fort Lancaster and Battlefield State Historic Site
629 Fort Lancaster Road, Sheffield, TX 79781
Fort Lancaster and Battlefield State Historic Site commemorates the vestiges of one of several posts established in the 1850s that played an important role in westward expansion by providing escorts for mail carriers, wagon trains, and settlers on the San Antonio–El Paso Road en route to California. Today, visitors wander through ruins imagining the once-impressive establishment of over 30 permanent buildings—including a blacksmith shop, hospital, sutler's store, and bakery.

Fort Martin Scott State Historic Site
1606 E. Main Street, Fredericksburg, TX 78624
This site offers an immersive experience through a blend of replica structures and original historic buildings, including the guard house and jail. Recognized as a State Archeological Landmark and listed in the National Register of Historic Places, Fort Martin Scott stands as a testament to the rich history of the region.

Fort McKavett State Historic Site
7066 FM 864, Fort McKavett, TX 76841
The remains of this 150-year-old West Texas fort is considered one of the best preserved and most intact examples of a Texas Indian Wars (1850–1875) military post. Restored structures include the officers' quarters, barracks, hospital, schoolhouse, dead house, sink, and post headquarters. In addition, there are ruins of several buildings, most notably the commanding officer's quarters and the barracks along the north side of the parade ground, which

once was the longest building west of the Mississippi River.

French Legation State Historic Site
802 San Marcos Street, Austin, TX 78702
One of the oldest houses in Austin, the French Legation opened in 1841 as a home and diplomatic outpost for the French chargé d'affaires to the Republic of Texas, Alphonse Dubois, after France recognized the Republic of Texas as a sovereign nation.

Fulton Mansion State Historic Site
317 S. Fulton Beach Road, Rockport, TX 78382
Fulton Mansion must have appeared incredible in 1877, as it does today, with its mansard roof and ornate trim. Interior gas lighting, flush-toilets, and other refinements were progressive and luxurious elements for this part of Texas history. Fulton Mansion is a Recorded Texas Historic Landmark and listed in the National Register of Historic Places.

Iwo Jima Museum and Monument State Historic Site
320 Iwo Jima Blvd., Harlingen, TX 78550
The Iwo Jima Monument stands as a powerful tribute to the heroic actions of six Marines on February 23, 1945, who raised an American flag atop Mount Suribachi during the Battle of Iwo Jima. Crafted by sculptor Dr. Felix W. de Weldon, the larger-than-life figures perfectly recreate the iconic flag-raising moment captured by photographer Joe Rosenthal, while the adjacent Iwo Jima Museum educates visitors about their valor and the drama of World War II's Pacific Theater.

Kreische Brewery State Historic Site
414 TX-92 Spur, La Grange, TX 78945
In 1849, German immigrant Heinrich Ludwig Kreische purchased 172 acres of land including the Dawson/Mier tomb, now known as Monument Hill State Historic Site. Master stonemason Kreische built a three-story house for his family. In the 1860s, he utilized the spring water from the ravine below his house and started one of the first commercial breweries in Texas. Walk the ruins of this once-bustling brewery and envision how Fayette County citizens would come and enjoy a pint of Kreische's Bluff Beer while looking out toward the beautiful Texas landscape. The Kreische Brewery and home are listed in the National Register of Historic Places.

Landmark Inn State Historic Site
402 Florence Street, Castroville, TX 78009
Landmark Inn tells the story of migration, industry, and preservation in Texas on the banks of the Medina River in the historic town of Castroville, known as "The Little Alsace of Texas." The site is a unique part of the San Antonio Metropolitan Area. Castroville, planned in 1844 as an exurb of San Antonio, it was just one day's wagon ride west (today just 25 minutes by car). It still operates today as a bed and breakfast facility.

Levi Jordan Plantation State Historic Site
10510 FM 524, Brazoria, TX 77422
Significant to the antebellum period of Texas history and the tumultuous era of Reconstruction, this site hosted a sizable plantation operation and two-story Greek Revival-style house. Levi Jordan moved his family and enslaved workers to Texas to establish a sugar and cotton plantation on the San Bernard River in the late 1840s. The site highlights the multiple perspectives and evolving relationships of those who lived and worked on the land during the 19th century. Today, the Levi Jordan Plantation provides a unique opportunity to understand the evolving agricultural history of the South and the early African American experience in Texas.

Lipantitlan State Historic Site
Lipantitlan Park Road, Sandia, TX 78383 Iwo Jima
Located in Nueces County near Sandia, this site was named after the Lipan Apaches that camped in the vicinity. In 1831, a picket fort was constructed by Mexican forces in anticipation of Anglo immigration. In 1835, the small guard force that held the fort surrendered it to the Texan forces without a shot being fired.

Magoffin Home State Historic Site
1120 Magoffin Avenue, El Paso, Texas 79901
Nestled in downtown El Paso, this striking and unique adobe homestead tells the stories of a multicultural family that influenced the development of the Southwest borderlands. Magoffin family members actively participated in American expansion, West Texas settlement, trade on the Santa Fe-Chihuahua Trail, Civil War turmoil, and U.S.-Mexico relations.

Mission Dolores State Historic Site
701 South Broadway Street, San Augustine, TX 75972
Mission Dolores was a Spanish mission built in 1721 in what is now San Augustine County, 20 miles west of the Texas-Louisiana border. There are no historic above-ground remains of the mission, but site was confirmed by archeological investigations and historical records. Mission Dolores is listed in the National Register of Historic Places and is a designated State Antiquities Landmark. El Camino Real de los Tejas National Historic Trail also passes through the property. Visitors can explore the site's history at the museum where interpretive displays tell the story of Mission Dolores.

Monument Hill State Historic Site
414 TX-92 Spur, La Grange, TX 78945
The monument marks the tomb of the men that died during the Dawson Massacre of September 1842 and the ill-fated Mier expedition of November 1842, which resulted in the March 1843 "black bean" incident. Nearby citizens reinterred their remains here in a common tomb so that they can be honored for their sacrifice. The site is now marked by a 1936 Centennial monument.

National Museum of the Pacific War State Historic Site
311 E. Austin Street, Fredericksburg, TX 78624
The National Museum of the Pacific War (NMPW) is recognized today as a world-class, cultural institution. A Smithsonian Affiliate and accredited by the American Alliance of Museums, NMPW provides the nation's most comprehensive account of World War II in the Asiatic-Pacific theater. Remaining true to its promise to Admiral Nimitz: to honor all who served and supported the war effort in the Pacific, the Museum proudly presents the facts, stories, and authentic artifacts of the Pacific War for today and generations to come.

Old Socorro Mission State Historic Site
10551 Nicholas Road, Socorro, TX 79927
The Old Socorro Mission site is a Franciscan mission named Nuestra Señora de La Limpia Concepción de los Piros de Socorro del Sur, founded in 1682 to serve Spanish families and Native American communities displaced from New Mexico during the Pueblo Revolt. The historical records detail not only the mission, but the Piro Pueblo that was established alongside it. Rebuilt at least four times, the mission was destroyed in 1829 by the flooding of the Rio Grande and was ultimately relocated. Nearby, the present-day mission and the Ysleta del Sur Pueblo, home of the descendants of the Puebloans, provide a direct link between the former site and the contemporary community.

Palmito Ranch Battlefield State Historic Site
43296 Palmito Hill Road, Brownsville, TX 78521
The Battle of Palmito Ranch was the final land battle of the American Civil War, fought May 12–13, 1865, along the banks of the Rio Grande. The battle, a Confederate victory, took place more than a month after Gen. Robert E. Lee's surrender of the Army of Northern Virginia to Union forces and 13 days before the Army of the Trans-Mississippi under Gen. Edmund Smith surrendered in Galveston on May 26.

Port Isabel Lighthouse State Historic Site
421 East Queen Isabella Blvd, Port Isabel, TX 78578
The lighthouse was built in 1852 due to the great number of shipwrecks that had occurred off Brazos Island in the Gulf of Mexico. By 1905, the lighthouse was decommissioned due to a downturn in maritime traffic caused by changes to the Rio Grande and the growth of railways. Present day, a reconstructed lighthouse keeper's cottage sits in the shadow of Port Isabel's 72-foot lighthouse and serves as a visitor center and museum.

Presidio La Bahía State Historic Site
217 Loop 71, Goliad, TX 77963
The Presidio, established in 1749 on this site during the Spanish colonial period, was crucial to the development of Texas. Witnessing filibustering expeditions and playing a role in the Mexican war for independence from Spain, the Presidio was the site of the Goliad Massacre on Palm Sunday, March 1836. It played host to one of the bloodiest chapters in Texas' quest for independence from Mexico after the shocking Texian defeat at the Battle of Coleto Creek. The massacre prompted the rallying cry, "Remember Goliad!" heard at the Battle of San Jacinto.

Sabine Pass Battleground State Historic Site
6100 Dowling Road, Port Arthur, TX 77655
The location of a significant Civil War battlefield, Sabine Pass Battleground State Historic Site tells the story of Confederate Lt. Richard "Dick" Dowling and his 46 men who thwarted a Union assault on Sabine Pass, a primary Texas port for Confederate shipments of supplies and vital to the war effort. In a battle lasting less than an hour, Dowling and his men destroyed two gunboats, resulting in significant casualties and the capture of nearly 350 prisoners.

Sam Bell Maxey House State Historic Site
812 South Church Street, Paris, TX 75460
Sam Bell Maxey was a Mexican War veteran, former Confederate general, and future U.S. Senator when his family moved into their fashionable, newly built home on the south side of Paris in 1868. In this home, the Maxey family navigated the political and social landscape from Reconstruction Era Texas through the start of the First World War.

Sam Rayburn House State Historic Site
890 W. State Hwy. 56 Bonham, TX 75418
One of the most powerful and influential politicians in the 20th century, Rayburn served in the U.S. Congress for 48 years, holding the position of speaker for 17 years. His 1916 home, now the Sam Rayburn House State Historic Site, preserves his real stories with original furnishings, candid photographs, and personal belongings, remaining as they were when he lived here. Visitors explore Rayburn's personal life and political achievements and their impact on mid-20th-century history.

San Felipe de Austin State Historic Site
220 2nd Street, San Felipe, TX 77473
Commemorating the location where, in 1823, Stephen F. Austin established a headquarters for his colony in Mexican Texas, San Felipe de Austin State Historic Site and museum share the stories of early settlers in this region. Today, visitors can walk in the footsteps of these early pioneers at what was the social, economic, and political center of American immigration to Texas before independence. San Felipe de Austin didn't survive the war for Texas independence—it was burned by its own residents as they evacuated during the Runaway Scrape of 1836.

San Jacinto Battleground State Historic Site
3523 Independence Parkway South, La Porte, TX 77571
On a chilly April afternoon in 1836, this strip of coastal prairie rang with the boom of cannon, crack of musket fire, and shouts of "Remember the Alamo!" and "Remember La Bahía!" Despite being outnumbered, Gen. Sam Houston's army of settlers, Tejanos, and foreign volunteers decisively defeated Gen. Antonio López de Santa Anna's forces and won Texas' independence. Today, the 1,200-acre site, San Jacinto Museum, and the 567-foot-tall San Jacinto Monument celebrate their sacrifice and victory.

Slaton Harvey House State Historic Site
400 Railroad Avenue, Slaton, TX 79364
Established in 1912, the Slaton Harvey House was originally one of several restaurants constructed along the Santa Fe Railway route. This beautiful example of Mission Revival architecture was designed by renowned architect Louis Curtiss, known as the "Frank Lloyd Wright of Kansas City." Today, the 1912 Slaton Harvey House is an historic one-of-a-kind bed and breakfast, event center, and railroad museum.

Star of the Republic Museum State Historic Site
23400 Park Rd 12, Washington, TX 77880
The Star of the Republic Museum was created by the Texas Legislature and is administered by the Texas Historical Commission as a cultural and educational institution. Its purpose is to collect and preserve the material culture of the Texas Republic (1836-1846) and to interpret the history, cultures, diversity, and values of early Texans. The museum is part of the Washington-on-the-Brazos State Historic Site complex.

Starr Family Home State Historic Site
407 West Travis Street, Marshall, TX 75670
Starr Family Home State Historic Site is composed of several elegant structures that map the 150-year history of the Starr family in Texas. Period furnishings, clothing, and antiques trace the transition of the buildings through four generations of the Starr family in Texas history.

Stephen F. Austin Memorial State Historic Site
900 Oil Field Road, West Columbia, TX 77486
A great lawn and marker indicate the home of George B. McKinstry where Stephen F. Austin, the Father of Texas, died on December 27, 1836.

Varner-Hogg Plantation State Historic Site
1702 N. 13th Street, West Columbia, TX 77486
Generations of Texas history, commerce, and entrepreneurship encapsulate Varner-Hogg Plantation State Historic Site, which tells the stories of the many families, both enslaved and not, who worked to build Texas. Over its 134-year history, the site hosted sugarcane production, cattle ranching, and oil drilling as it transitioned through the ownership of the Varners, the Pattons, and the Hoggs.

Washington-on-the-Brazos State Historic Site
23400 Park Rd 12, Washington, TX 77880
People revere Washington-on-the-Brazos State Historic Site as the site of the signing of the Texas Declaration of Independence on March 2, 1836. The Star of the Republic Museum, Independence Hall, the Washington Townsite, and Barrington Living History Farm offer the visitor a unique insight into the lives of the people who established the Republic of Texas.

Zaragoza Birthplace State Historic Site
217 Loop 71, Goliad, TX 77963
On May 5, 1862, in the Mexican city of Puebla, Zaragoza and his soldiers overpowered French expedition forces in the Battle of Puebla. The victory helped solidify President Benito Juarez's reform movement, which was organized to resist French occupation of Mexico and restore the Mexican Republic. Today, the victory is celebrated in both Mexico and the United States and is commonly known as Cinco de Mayo.

Recipe By Site

NOTES

NOTES

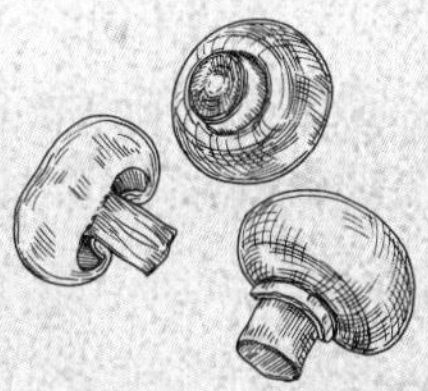

Historic Cookbooks

The Manuscript of Ann Maria Morris, Ann Marie Morris, 1824
The Virgina Housewife, Mary Rabdolph, 1824
The Cook's Oracle, William Kitchiner, 1829
The Cook's Own Book, Mrs. N. K. M. Lee, 1832
Domestic French Cookery, Chiefly Translated from Sulpice Barué, Miss Eliza Leslie, 1836
The Kentucky Housewife, Lettice Bryan, 1839
Domestic Cookery, Useful Receipts, and Hints to Young Housekeepers, Elizabeth Ellicott Lea, 1845
The Housekeeper's Assistant, Anna H Allen, 1845
The Southern Gardener and Receipt Book, P. Thornton, 1845
The Carolina Housewife, Sarah Rutledge, 1847
The American Matron- Practical and Scientific Cookery, A. Housekeeper, 1851
Mrs. Chadwick's Home Cookery, Mrs. J. Chadwick, 1853
Miss Leslie's New Receipts for Cookery, Eliza Leslie, 1854
Every Lady's Cook Book, Mrs. T. J. Crowen, 1856
Mrs. Beeton's Book of Household Management, Isabella Beeton, 1861
What Mrs. Fisher knows about Old Southern Cooking, Soups, Pickles, Preserves, Etc., Abby Fisher, 1881
Miss Parola's New Cook Book, Maria Parola, 1882
The Texas Cookbook: A Thorough Treatise on the Art of Cookery, 1883
Practical American Cookery and Household Management, Julia Corson, 1886
Lessons in Cookery, First Mission School of Cookery & Housework, Mrs. Anna Lowell Woodbury, 1889
Manual of Domestic Work- Practical Lessons in Cookery, Anna Woodbury, 1889
The Bread and Biscuit Baker's and Sugar-Boiler's Assistant, Robert Wells, 1890
The El Paso Cook Book, 1898
The Encyclopedia of Practical Cookery, Theodore Francis Garrett, 1898.
The Enterprising Housekeeper, Ellen Louise Johnson, 1898
German Cookery, Ella Oswald, 1906
The Knights of Pythias Oakleaf Temple No. 41 Cookbook, Lyra, TX, 1907
Super Chef Cook Book of Famous Fred Harvey Recipes, Santa Fe Railroad, 1924
Fannin County Home Demonstration Club Cookbook published in 1933
Better Homes and Gardens, December, 1958

BIBLIOGRAPHY

Baker, C. *Tex-Mex: The Cookbook*. San Francisco: Chronicle Books, 1999.

Beeton, Isabella. *The Book of Household Management*. London: Ex-classics Project, 1861.

Farmer, Fannie Merritt. *The Boston Cooking-School Cook Book*. Boston: Little, Brown, and Company, 1905.

HathiTrust Digital Library. *Hathitrust Digital Library - Cookbooks*. https://www.hathitrust.org/.

Haven, Alice B. *Personal Reminiscences of Miss Eliza Leslie*. Godey's Lady's Book 56 1858.

Leslie, Eliza. *Directions for Cookery, in its Various Branches*. Philadelphia: E.L. Carey & Hart, 1840.

Leslie, Eliza. *Domestic French Cookery*. Philadelphia: Carey & Hart, 1836.

Leslie, Eliza. *The Lady's Receipt-Book: A Useful Companion for Large or Small Families*. Philadelphia: E.L. Carey & Hart, 1847, c1846.

Longone, Janice B. and Daniel T. *American Cookbooks and Wine Books 1797-1950*. Ann Arbor, Michigan, 1984.

López, D. *The Tex-Mex Cookbook: A History in Recipes and Photos*. Austin: University of Texas Press, 2004.

McWilliams, J. *The Foodways of Texas: A History of the Lone Star State's Culinary Heritage*. College Station: Texas A&M University Press, 2014.

Michigan State University. *Feeding America: The Historic American Cookbook Project*. https://d.lib.msu.edu/fa.

Morgan, Sarah. *The Saga of Texas Cookery*. Austin: The Encino Press, 1973.

Oliver, Lynne. *The Food Timeline*. https://www.foodtimeline.org/index.html.

Pfaelzer, Jean. *American National Biography*. Vol. 13. Eds. John A. Garraty and Mark C. Carnes. New York: Oxford, 1999.

Russell, Malinda. *Domestic Cook Book: Containing a Careful Selection of Useful Receipts for the Kitchen*. Paw Paw, MI: Self-published, 1866.

Russell, Malinda. *Malinda Russell: African American Cook and Author*, 1866. https://malindarussell.com/background-info.

Smith, Joanne. *Cuisine, Texas: A Multicultural Feast*. Austin: University of Texas Press, 1995.

The Institute of Texas Cultures. The Melting Pot: Ethnic Cuisine in Texas. San Antonio: The Institute of Texas Cultures, 1977.

Vaughn, Daniel. *"Is Elgin's Southside Market the Oldest Barbeque Joint in Texas? The Saga Continues."* Texas Monthly, September 26, 2022.

Weiser-Alexander, Kathy. *Legends of America: Chuckwagon- Western Recipes*. https://www.legendsofamerica.com/we-oldwestrecipes/.

INGREDIENT INDEX

A

B

C

N

O

P

Q

R